SHARKS & RAYS
OF THE WORLD

Printed in Hong Kong

99 00 01 02 03 5 4 3 2 1

Library of Congress Cataloging-in-Publication Data
Perrine, Doug.
Sharks and rays of the world / Doug Perrine.
p.   cm.
Includes bibliographical references.
Summary: Examines the natural history and evolution of various
species of sharks and rays, members of the same subclass, describing
their physical characteristics, feeding, reproduction, human
encounters, and more.
ISBN 0-89658-448-8
1. Sharks Juvenile literature.   2. Rays (Fishes) Juvenile literature.
[1. Sharks   2. Rays (Fishes)]   I. Title.
QL638.9.P437   1999
597.3—dc21   99-25791
                                                                          CIP

Distributed in Canada by Raincoast Books, 8680 Cambie Street, Vancouver, B.C. V6P 6M9

Published by Voyageur Press, Inc.
123 North Second Street, P.O. Box 338, Stillwater, MN 55082 U.S.A.
651-430-2210, fax 651-430-2211

Educators, fundraisers, premium and gift buyers, publicists, and marketing managers:
Looking for creative products and new sales ideas? Voyageur Press books are available at special
discounts when purchased in quantities, and special editions can be created to your
specifications. For details contact the marketing department at 800-888-9653.

All photography supplied by Innerspace Visions / Photography copyright © 1999 by

Page 1 © Rudie Kuiter
Page 3 © Mark Strickland
Page 4 © Doug Perrine
Page 8 © Bob Cranston
Page 10 © Doug Perrine
Page 12 © Doug Perrine
Page 13 © Doug Perrine
Page 14 © Doug Perrine
Page 15 © Doug Perrine
Page 16 © James D. Watt
Page 18 © Steve Drogin
Page 19 © Mark Conlin
Page 20 © Steve Drogin
Page 22 Top Left © Ray Troll
Page 22 Top Right © Ray Troll
Page 22 Bottom Left © Ray Troll
Page 22 Bottom Right © Ray Troll
Page 23 © Ivy Rutzky
Page 25 © Doug Perrine
Page 26 © David B. Fleetham
Page 27 © Ray Troll

Page 29 © Doug Perrine
Page 30 © Saul Gonor
Page 33 © Howard Hall
Page 35 © Doug Perrine
Page 36 © Doug Perrine
Page 39 © Doug Perrine
Page 40 © Doug Perrine
Page 42 © Mark Conlin
Page 45 © Doug Perrine
Page 46 © Howard Hall
Page 48 © David B. Fleetham
Page 49 © Gary Bell
Page 50 © David B. Fleetham
Page 53 © Richard Herrmann
Page 55 © Ben Cropp
Page 56 © Mark Conlin
Page 59 © David B. Fleetham
Page 60 © David B. Fleetham
Page 63 © James D. Watt
Page 64 © Howard Hall
Page 67 © Marty Snyderman

Page 68 © Marty Snyderman
Page 71 © Doug Perrine
Page 72 © James D. Watt
Page 75 Left © Doug Perrine
Page 75 Right © Doug Perrine
Page 76 © Tom Campbell
Page 79 © Nigel Marsh
Page 83 © David Fleetham
Page 84 © James D. Watt
Page 87 Top Left © A & A Ferrari
Page 87 Top Right © Doug Perrine
Page 87 Bottom Left © David Wrobel
Page 87 Bottom Right © Gary Adkison
Page 89 © David B. Fleetham
Page 91 © Tom Haight
Page 92 © Howard Hall
Page 95 © Howard Hall
Page 96 © Doug Perrine
Page 99 © Mark Conlin
Page 100 © Doug Perrine
Page 103 © Doug Perrine

Page 104 © Saul Gonor
Page 107 Top Left © Doug Perrine
Page 107 Top Right © David Wrobel
Page 107 Bottom Left © Rudie Kuiter
Page 107 Bottom Right © Florian Graner
Page 108 © Mark Conlin
Page 111 © Marty Snyderman
Page 112 © Doug Perrine
Page 115 © Doug Perrine
Page 116 © Doug Perrine
Page 117 Right © Phillip Colla
Page 117 Top Left © Doug Perrine
Page 117 Bottom Left © Richard Herrmann
Page 118 Top © Mark Strickland
Page 118 Bottom © Doug Perrine
Page 121 © Phillip Colla
Page 122 © Doug Perrine
Page 125 © David B. Fleetham
Page 127 © Doug Perrine
Page 131 © Doug Perrine

Front cover © Doug Perrine   Back cover top © Steve Drogin   Back cover bottom © Doug Perrine

SHARKS & RAYS
OF THE WORLD

Doug Perrine

Voyageur Press

Contents

Evolutionary Relationships of Sharks and Rays

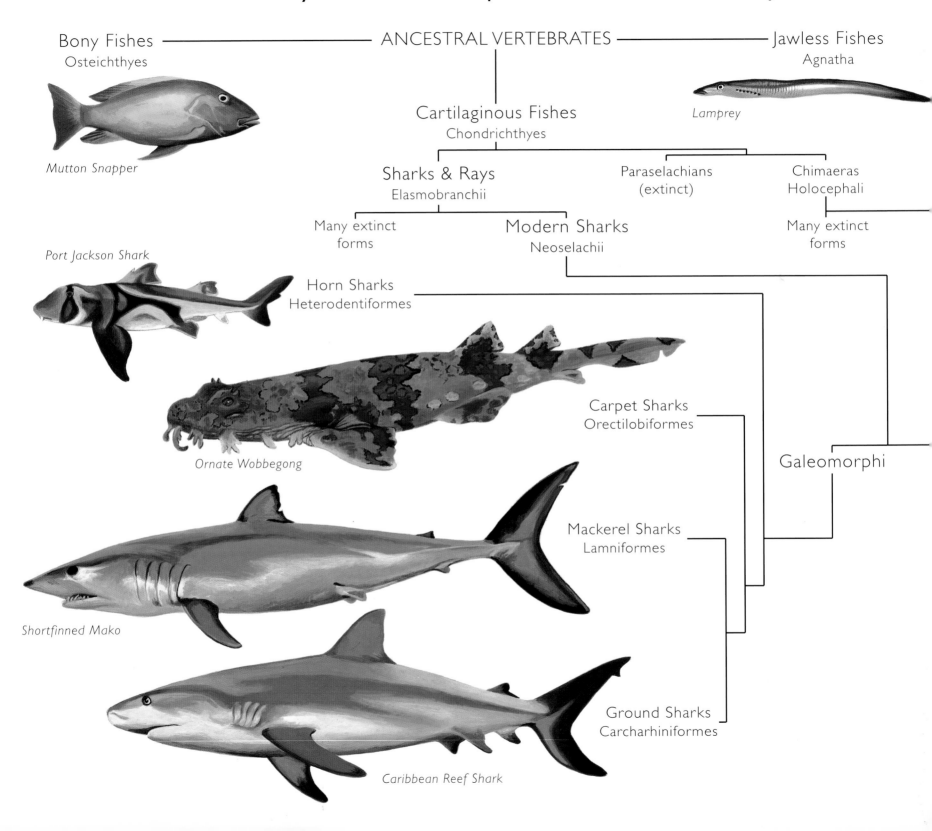

Bony Fishes
Osteichthyes

Mutton Snapper

ANCESTRAL VERTEBRATES

Jawless Fishes
Agnatha

Lamprey

Cartilaginous Fishes
Chondrichthyes

Sharks & Rays
Elasmobranchii

Paraselachians
(extinct)

Chimaeras
Holocephali

Many extinct forms

Modern Sharks
Neoselachii

Many extinct forms

Port Jackson Shark

Horn Sharks
Heterodentiformes

Carpet Sharks
Orectilobiformes

Ornate Wobbegong

Galeomorphi

Mackerel Sharks
Lamniformes

Shortfinned Mako

Ground Sharks
Carcharhiniformes

Caribbean Reef Shark

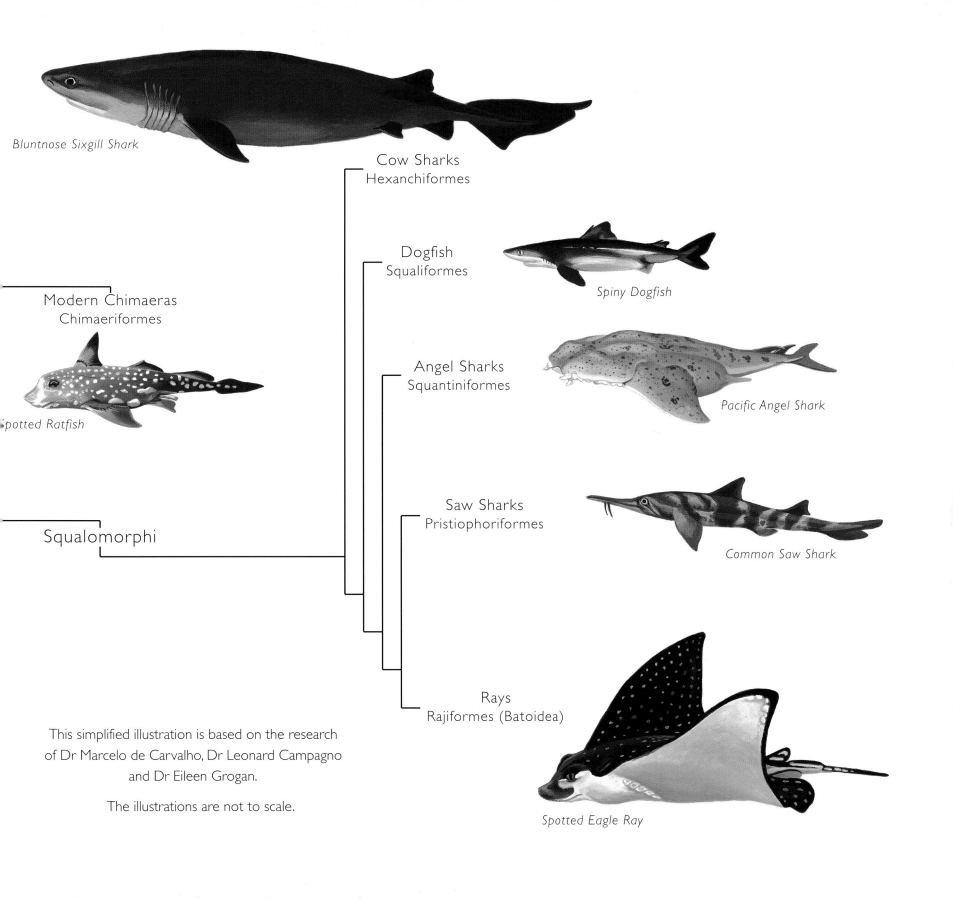

Bluntnose Sixgill Shark

Cow Sharks
Hexanchiformes

Modern Chimaeras
Chimaeriformes

Spotted Ratfish

Dogfish
Squaliformes

Spiny Dogfish

Squalomorphi

Angel Sharks
Squantiniformes

Pacific Angel Shark

Saw Sharks
Pristiophoriformes

Common Saw Shark

Rays
Rajiformes (Batoidea)

This simplified illustration is based on the research
of Dr Marcelo de Carvalho, Dr Leonard Campagno
and Dr Eileen Grogan.

The illustrations are not to scale.

Spotted Eagle Ray

Introduction

In the brief period since my first book, *Sharks*, was published in 1995, an almost miraculous change has occurred in the way that many people think of sharks. From perhaps the first day that humans ventured out upon the ocean right up through the 1980s, sharks have been vilified as bloodthirsty monsters with an insatiable craving for human flesh. Fear and loathing of sharks reached hysterical levels after the release of the film *Jaws*, causing a number of people to give up swimming and other marine recreations, and resulting in the senseless slaughter of untold numbers of sharks. Animosity toward rays was less intense, but many people equated all rays with stingrays, and considered them as a public menace, while mantas were known as 'devilfish', and greatly feared by some.

Over the last few years, however, sharks and rays have been largely de-mythologized in public perception. People are now more likely to see them as magnificent predators than as menacing monsters.

Concurrently, large international markets have developed for shark fins, cartilage, meat, and hides. The rapidly rising value of shark products has triggered an explosive growth in fisheries for sharks and rays which threatens to drive many populations into commercial extinction. With the new recognition of sharks and rays as wildlife, rather than demons, has come an acceptance of the fact that, like all wildlife under exploitation, populations must be managed if they are to continue to exist. Conservation groups have sprung up dedicated primarily to the preservation of these groups of fishes, something I could have barely imagined just a decade ago.

Another event I could never have foreseen back in the days when the word 'shark' was synonymous with 'man-eater', and the very mention of sharks was taboo in the recreational diving industry, is the development of shark and ray encounters as popular recreational activities. The public fascination with these animals has led even to the appearance of shark calendars next to the calendars of swimsuit models in book stores.

While we have come a long way in the last few years, a number of myths still remain. The popular perception of a shark is still something akin to *Tyrannosaurus rex*. They are considered to be living fossils – perfect predators, unchanged for 400 million years. Many otherwise reasonable people believe for some reason that the laws of natural selection do not apply to sharks. While it is true that the rate of morphological change of sharks and rays has not equaled the explosive adaptive radiation of mammals, the idea that they have ceased to evolve is ridiculous. In fact, sharks and rays have undergone extensive change from their earliest fossil ancestors, and have evolved into a fascinating array of widely varied forms. Particularly in terms of sensory and reproductive adaptations, they can be regarded as among the most highly evolved of all the fishes. Some types of bony fishes are considered more primitive than any modern shark (meaning that they share more characteristics with a very early ancestor).

In this book I will discuss some of the fascinating adaptations that sharks and their kin have evolved, and endeavor to show how these unique features suit their varied lifestyles. Indeed, this group of animals has diversified into so many different forms, with so many interesting and sometimes bizarre features, that it is impossible to consider all of them in a volume of this size. If their size and habitat didn't render them so terribly difficult to study, perhaps Darwin would have devoted more of his career to them, instead of spending so much of it on barnacles. In recent years, modern technologies have begun to revolutionize the study of these animals, such as data recorders that can be attached to a free-swimming shark, and transmit back all sorts of physiological and environmental data. With any luck, so much will be learned in the next decade or two that this book will become nearly obsolete.

What are Sharks and Rays?

Sharks, rays, and their allies belong to the class Chondrichthyes, one of three major groups of fishes. Like all fishes, they have a spinal chord, and are therefore part of the phylum Chordata, along with mammals, reptiles, birds, and amphibians. Chondrichthyans are differentiated from other fishes by having jaws, skeletons which are composed primarily of cartilage, rather than bone, and, in the males only, a unique set of appendages called claspers between the pelvic fins.

The other two groups of fish are the jawless fishes (Agnatha) and the bony fishes (Osteichthyes). The jawless fishes – lampreys and hagfish – have cartilaginous skeletons, but no jaws or claspers. There are about 88 living species.

The bony fishes are by far the largest of the three groups of fish, with about 24,000 species. They have jaws, but no claspers, and their skeletons are made of bone. They shared a common ancestor with the chondrichthyans well over 400 million years ago. Since that time, the two groups have had separate evolutionary histories.

There are more than 1000 species of chondrichthyans known. This class is composed of two subclasses. The subclass Holocephali contains about 40 species of fishes known variously as chimaeras, ratfish, ghost sharks, elephantfish, spookfish, or rabbitfish. These are strange-looking animals that live mostly in deep water. While the skeleton is cartilaginous, the upper jaw is fused to the skull, as opposed to sharks and rays, which have loosely attached protrusile jaws. Unlike other chondrichthyans, chimaeras have no scales, and have tooth plates instead of individual teeth. The tooth plates are not replaced regularly, as are the teeth of sharks and rays. The first dorsal (back) fin can be raised and lowered, unlike those of sharks and rays, and is equipped with a sharp spine, which is often venomous. In addition to the pelvic claspers found in all chondrichthyans, the male chimaera has a set of prepelvic

claspers of unknown function and a frontal clasper on the head, which is used to hold onto the female during mating.

Sharks and rays belong to the subclass Elasmobranchii. This subclass is divided into eight orders of sharks, and one order of rays. The rays are closely allied with the flat-bodied angel sharks and saw sharks. In general a ray is a flat-bodied shark with expanded pectoral (side) fins that attach to the head forward of the gill slits. The gill slits are on the underside, rather than the sides of the head, and it swims by flapping or undulating its pectoral fins, rather than with the tail. However the divisions are not always clear-cut. Guitarfishes (rays), electric rays, and sawfishes (rays) all have their gill slits underneath but swim with their tails like sharks. Angel sharks have their gills on the underside, and are flattened, with broad pectoral fins, like rays, but the pectoral fins do not attach to the head, as they do in rays. Some authorities just refer to rays as 'pancake sharks'. Most of the statements made about sharks in this book apply equally to rays.

At this writing, there are 409 species of sharks recognized, and 560 species of 'batoid elasmobranchs' (rays, skates, sawfishes, and guitarfishes). The word 'rays' in this book will normally refer to all of the batoids. Additionally over 100 species of sharks and rays have been photographed or collected, but not scientifically described and named, and an unknown number are still awaiting discovery. Elasmobranchs exhibit a tremendous diversity of body forms and lifestyles, but there are a number of characteristics which they all share.

All sharks and rays are carnivores, or flesh eaters. Not all are predators. Some are filter-feeders, sifting small plankton out of the water. Others grub in the sand for shellfish. But none are herbivores (vegetarians). They have evolved the ability to sling the jaws forward while feeding. This is made possible by the fact that the upper jaw is not fused to the skull, as it is in chimaeras and in the more primitive groups

Rays are just flat-bodied sharks with head, body, and pectoral fins joined together and gills underneath. Southern stingray (Dasyatis americana).

*The large first dorsal fins of sharks and rays are stiff and permanently erect, unlike those
of chimaeras and bony fish, which are folded flat against the body when not in use. All of the fins of
elasmobranchs are stiffened and supported by collagen fibers which, when processed, form the essential
ingredient in shark-fin soup. The dorsal fins stabilize the body against sideways roll while swimming.
This fin belongs to a tiger shark, Galeocerdo cuvier, swimming just below the surface.*

of bony fishes. The embryonic origin and type of suspension of the jaw parts are different in sharks than in bony fishes. The efficiency of this arrangement enables some types of sharks to bite off pieces from prey much larger than themselves – an ability which is rare in the bony fishes.

Like all fishes, elasmobranchs 'breathe' by extracting oxygen from water with their gills. Water is taken in through the mouth, or in some cases through a modified gill opening known as a spiracle, and passed out through five to seven gill slits which are visible on the side (sharks) or underside (rays). In contrast, bony fishes and chimaeras have the gills hidden under a gill cover. Chimaeras draw water in for respiration through their nostrils, rather than their mouths. In elasmobranchs the nostrils are not connected to the respiratory system and are used only for smelling.

Most bony fishes have an organ called a swim bladder which they can inflate with air or other gases to regulate their buoyancy. Elasmobranchs have no swim bladders. Some achieve neutral or nearly neutral buoyancy by storing large amounts of low-density oil in their livers, while others depend upon the hydrodynamic lift (generated by their fins and heads as they swim) to counteract the pull of gravity.

The skin of sharks and rays is also unique. Bony fishes may have naked skin, as do chimaeras and agnathans, or may be covered with one of several types of scales. However, placoid scales are found only on elasmobranchs. Placoid scales are smaller than most other scales, and have a unique feature: a tiny dermal denticle, or 'tooth' on each scale. This structure is formed from the same type of tissue as the teeth in the mouth, and is even covered with dentine. It was once believed that small pits next to the dermal denticles contained taste buds, and that sharks could 'taste' with their skin, but this has proven to be untrue. It is true, though, that the skin can cause abrasion injuries. The denticles are generally pointed towards the rear of the body, so that the skin feels much rougher when rubbed from back to front, than in the other direction. Smaller fish sometimes take advantage of this by rubbing themselves 'against the grain' of a shark's skin to remove external parasites. The dermal denticles certainly improve an elasmobranch's

defense against predation and parasitism by increasing the strength of the skin, but the primary function is probably to increase hydrodynamic efficiency by reducing turbulence as the animal swims. In bottom-dwelling batoids, the placoid scales may be reduced to a few patches of armor, or to spines (including the 'stings' of stingrays).

The fins of elasmobranchs also differ from those of bony fishes,

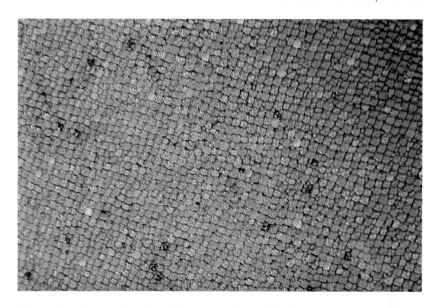

Placoid scales on the skin of a nurse shark (Ginglymostoma cirratum).

chimaeras, and jawless fishes. Instead of thin, flexible fins, which are supported by spines and fin rays, sharks and rays have thick fins which are stiffened by internal fibers of collagen. Their fins have a limited range of movement compared to the fins of most bony fishes. They cannot fold any of their fins flat against the body or conceal them in grooves, as many bony fishes can. The pectoral (side) fins of most sharks are shaped like airplane wings, and function in the same way, to provide lift, while additional lift and propulsion are furnished by the caudal (tail) fin. In batoids, the pectoral fins are modified into even larger 'wings', which are utilized by a number of species in a flapping motion to enable the ray to 'fly' through the water somewhat like a bird.

The most defining characteristic of the chondrichthyans is the cartilaginous skeleton. Cartilage is a connective tissue which is an embryonic precursor to bone. Humans retain small amounts of cartilage into adulthood, as the strengthening tissue in the nose and ears, for example. The primary advantage of having a skeleton of cartilage is reduced density. Cartilage is not nearly as heavy as bone; an important consideration, given the lack of a swim bladder in chondrichthyans.

Most of the fossil record of sharks consists only of teeth.

Parts of the skeletons of sharks and rays, such as the vertebrae, jaws, and parts of the skulls, are strengthened by the deposition of calcium compounds. These parts are hard and inflexible. The ability of some sharks to flex their heads around by their tails, often attributed to the cartilaginous skeleton, is actually due more to characteristics of the tendons and ligaments, as well as the number and arrangement of the hard-as-bone vertebrae. Although superficially similar to bone, this calcified cartilage has a different structure and composition from true bone. Unfortunately for our understanding of the evolutionary history of this fascinating group of animals, it is not nearly as easily fossilized as bone.

Much of the fossil record of elasmobranchs consists of teeth. This is not only because they are hard and easily preserved, but also because they are produced in prodigious numbers. Unlike bony fish and chimaeras, sharks and rays replace their functional teeth continuously. Rows of replacement teeth line up in the jaws on a 'conveyor belt' system, slowly moving forward to replace the working teeth, which drop off, so the shark is never stuck for long with broken or worn teeth.

Perhaps the most significant difference between the cartilaginous and bony fishes is the presence of claspers in the chondrichthyans. The importance of these paired male organs is in the mode of reproduction that they represent. The claspers are inserted (one at a time) into the female to deliver sperm into her body. All chondrichthyans reproduce by means of internal fertilization, whereas the vast majority of bony fishes practice external fertilization, with eggs and sperm being expelled from the body in an act known as 'spawning'. Sharks, rays, and chimaeras mate, rather than spawn. In many species this leads to live birth of the offspring – an advanced evolutionary characteristic found primarily in mammals.

Finally, an interesting, but not definitive, characteristic of the elasmobranchs is the large brain size. The brain to body weight ratio varies between species, and overlaps the range found in other fishes, but is higher than in most bony fishes. It corresponds more closely with relative brain sizes of small mammals. This may be related to the fact that most sharks are not able to sleep, an ability of mammals and some fishes that enables the brain to function more efficiently.

Brain size is not necessarily a direct indicator of intelligence. However, several experiments and many anecdotal observations indicate that these are intelligent fish that learn quickly. Certainly they are fascinating and have many remarkable abilities which deserve our respect and interest, and should inspire a responsible stewardship in place of the blind fear and mindless slaughter which is unfortunately not confined only to the past.

Sharks and rays have five, six or seven exposed gill slits, while in bony fishes and chimaeras the gills are covered by a hard plate.

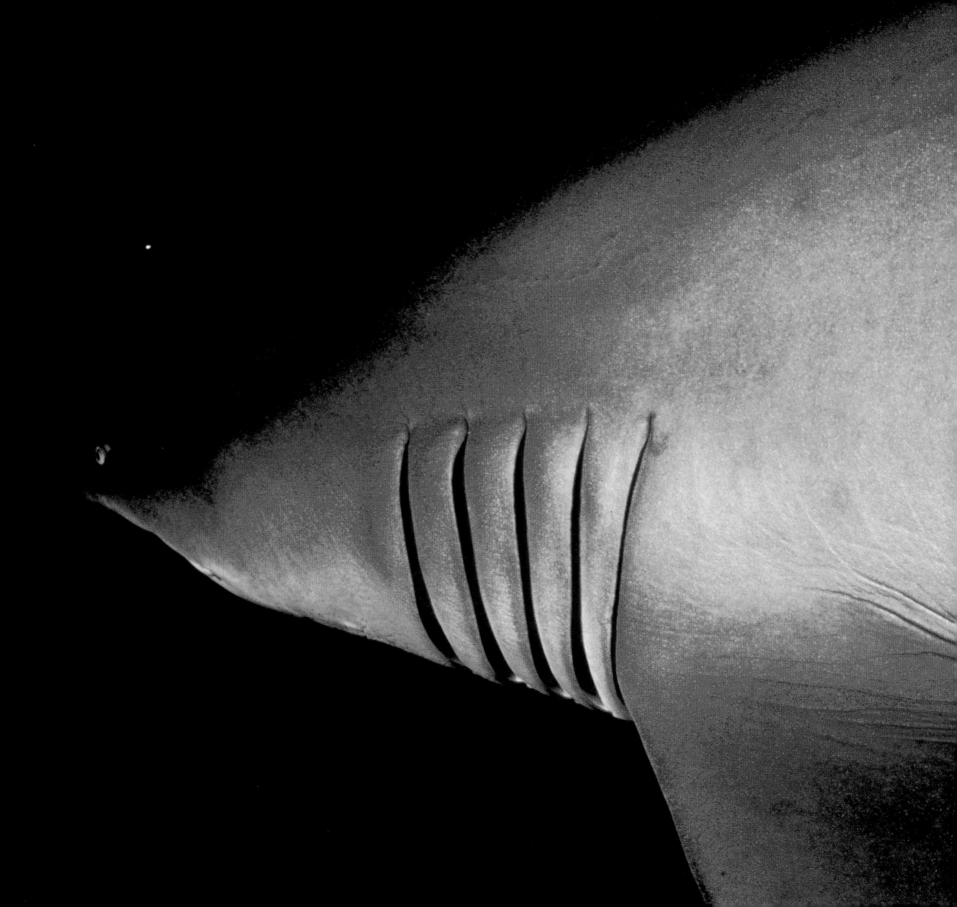

Origins and Ancestors

In paleontological circles, great debate rages about the origin of birds, sometime around 120 MYA (million years ago). The controversy is heated concerning the origins of humans, only 4–6 MYA. Therefore it should not be surprising that there are few clear and incontestable facts regarding the evolutionary history of fish, which appeared nearly 500 MYA. The uncertainty is due to the incompleteness of the fossil record. The gaps in the vertebrate record are worst in the case of the cartilaginous fishes (Chondrichthyes) due to the fact that the skeletons usually disintegrate after death. In only a few rare cases have impressions of entire shark bodies been preserved by sudden burial in mud. Most of the evolutionary record of the elasmobranchs consists of only teeth, scales, and vertebrae – the only parts hard enough to be consistently preserved. Although the cartilaginous skeletons are hardened by calcium deposits, these are laid down as a mosaic on the surface of the skeleton, and shatter into tiny individual prisms after the death of the animal. The soft cartilage then decomposes or is consumed by scavengers. Quite a few species of extinct sharks are known only from a single tooth. Many prehistoric sharks – possibly the majority – doubtless remain entirely unknown to us. As a result, there are no easy answers and little agreement when it comes to describing the evolutionary pathway that has led to modern elasmobranchs.

One thing that is certain is that sharks have continued to evolve throughout their history. Popular mythology suggests that sharks have remained unchanged for more than 400 million years – a silly notion given credence by endless repetition. In fact, the earliest sharks were considerably different from modern forms. They evolved into a great variety of forms, some of which were quite bizarre, and also distinct from present-day elasmobranchs. Most of these died off about 240 MYA, leaving only a few groups of chondrichthyans, also unlike those which exist today. Most of these died off 65 MYA. Before vanishing into extinction, some spawned the predecessors of modern elasmobranchs.

Most of the modern families of sharks and rays had their origins 150 to 25 MYA. Since the appearance of these families, the body shape of most sharks has not changed much, as far as we can tell from a fossil record that is based mostly on teeth. This tells us little about changes that might have occurred in the internal organs, chemistry, physiology, and behavior of the animals. Still, even 25 million years is a long time to keep the same kind of body, compared to the changes that have taken place in mammals since they burst on the scene a little over 200 MYA.

Rapid evolutionary change is expected when a group of animals begins to occupy new ecological niches, or when the environment changes. Indications are that elasmobranchs have occupied about the same ecological niche, broadly speaking, for quite some time. Additionally, the aquatic environment they occupy has been relatively stable, compared to terrestrial environments, until quite recently. Therefore it is expected that in recent evolutionary history, modifications would have occurred at a slower rate than in mammals. Terrestrial habitats have undergone drastic changes over the last 100 MY, with ice ages coming and going, continents drifting and colliding, volcanoes erupting and spewing gases into the atmosphere, gigantic meteorites smashing into the earth, and dominant groups of megafauna (such as dinosaurs) going extinct. Additionally, since their appearance, mammals have spread rapidly into new habitats, leading to a divergence of forms through a process known as 'adaptive radiation'.

A similar radiation took place in the chondrichthyan fishes after their appearance, during the period from approximately 400 to 300 MYA, as they evolved to take advantage of the different habitats that were available in the aquatic realm. At this time, warm, shallow seas covered

*A whale shark (*Rhincodon typus)*, the biggest fish in the world.*

much of what is now Europe and North America. Sharks and their relatives flourished, and evolved into many specialized forms, achieving a diversity comparable to present-day bony fishes. The bony fishes at this time were still relatively unspecialized. We can presume that the rate of chondrichthyan evolution slowed as the available habitats and niches were filled. This does not mean that sharks have 'stopped evolving'.

A coral cat shark (Atelomycterus marmoratus) *in Indonesia.*

There is, however, some evidence that the rate of evolution in sharks may be inherently lower than in mammals. This is indicated by a lower rate of spontaneous mutation, possibly 5 to 10 times lower, in the mitochondrial DNA. Natural selection acts on genetic variation, which arises from mutation. Less mutation produces less variation, and therefore slower evolution. If these studies are correct, sharks make fewer 'mistakes' when copying their mitochondrial DNA than do mammals.

Many of the present-day families of bony fishes arose in the late Cretaceous – the same period as the requiem sharks, the group containing most of the familiar reef sharks. By contrast, the cat sharks, cow sharks, and bullhead sharks are much older groups – dating back to the Jurassic. However, some of the bony fishes, such as lungfishes, have undergone little external evolution for a much longer period. They are very similar to ancestors that were alive before the age of dinosaurs!

Although rates of evolution (which can be measured in many different ways) may vary, in a sense all fish (and all animals) are the same age. They are all descended from the same ancestor in the distant past. We can be fairly certain that all modern vertebrates are descended from early jawless fishes, or agnathans. Present-day agnathans (lampreys and hagfish), however, are believed to be derived from different groups of early agnathans than jawed fishes (bony fishes and chondrichthyans). The ancestors of chondrichthyans may have belonged to the group of jawless fishes called thelodonts.

There is some evidence that the Chondrichthyes had a more recent ancestor among the early group of jawed fishes (placoderms). These were strange-looking flattened fishes with bony skeletons and plates of bony armor covering the outside of their bodies. The placoderms were in some cases so bizarre, that some researchers believe they were not all related to each other. Some were fearsome predators, attaining lengths of up to 33 ft (10 m). At least one kind of placoderm had claspers, and practiced internal fertilization, like the Chondrichthyes. There were still placoderms around when the first sharks appeared, and they probably fed on those early sharks. The placoderms radiated into a number of different forms which dominated the seas for a brief (geologically speaking) period before they disappeared suddenly and completely, leaving a void which was rapidly filled by the evolution of sharks into new forms.

The first sharks may have appeared 450 or more MYA. We know nothing about these early chondrichthyans because they left no teeth, and no skeletal parts. All that remains of them are tiny scales. However, these scales are so similar to those of later sharks, that there is no doubt they came from sharks. Why have no teeth been found from this early period? 'It may be that sharks evolved before their teeth', says Dr John Maisey, of the American Museum of Natural History. In fact the earliest fossil teeth come from strata 40 to 70 million years younger.

During embryonic development, the mouth of a shark is formed from an inward fold of the skin. It is likely that dentine-covered spines (dermal

Sharks have evolved in concert with their prey, maintaining a balance between predator and prey.
This whitetip reef shark (Triaenodon obesus) is a requiem shark, belonging to the family Carcharhinidae,
which first appeared about 63 million years ago, after the disappearance of the dinosaurs.

denticles) first evolved on the placoid scales on the outside of sharks' bodies, then spread into their mouths, where they proved to be useful in handling food. Gradually, the denticles on the jaw began to develop into forms that were distinct from those on the body, and to increase in size to improve food-processing capabilities. The 'missing links' or 'proto-teeth' may have already been discovered. Some denticles have been found which are slightly larger than the skin denticles, but are otherwise identical. Perhaps these formed on the jaws of those very early sharks.

The oldest shark fossil consisting of more than teeth and scales dates from about 380 MYA. It was named *Antarctilamna*, because the first example was discovered in Antarctica. A braincase and fin spines have been found in addition to teeth. The bicuspid teeth are similar to those of the later xenacanths, and the fin spines are similar to those of the ctenacanths so it may be ancestral to either or both groups.

The ctenacanths ('comb spines' in Greek) appeared about 10 MY later. In addition to teeth with a large sharp primary cusp and smaller side cusps, they had two spines in front of each dorsal fin which were covered with nodules, giving them a comblike appearance. They lasted for 80 MY, and are considered by Dr Maisey to be the most likely candidate for the ancestral group to all of the Mesozoic and modern sharks.

About this time, 370 MYA, another group appeared, known as cladodonts ('branched teeth') whose multi-cusped teeth were similar to those of the ctenacanths. These were not replaced regularly, as are those of modern sharks, and consequently exhibit signs of wear. Some cladodonts are known only from the teeth, but one, dubbed *Cladoselache*, achieved fame by being buried in the sediments on the bottom of the shallow sea which covered much of what is now North America. The sediments hardened into shales, which have preserved impressions of *Cladoselache*, skin, muscles, internal organs, stomach contents, and all.

Cladoselache attained lengths of nearly 6½ ft (2 m). Its form was shark-like, with a streamlined body, two dorsal fins (front and rear) on top, paired pectoral (side) and pelvic (underside) fins, and a large tail. The tail was crescent-shaped, like those of tunas and other fast-swimming fish, and obviously designed for speed. It needed speed both to escape the giant armored fish which preyed upon it, and also to capture its own prey. It chased down smaller fish and swallowed them tail first, through a mouth which was located at the front of its snout, rather than underneath as in most of today's sharks. A spine in front of each dorsal fin probably provided added protection against consumption by the armored fish which must have lunged up from the bottom to seize it – much as bottom-dwelling angel sharks sometimes snap up small horn sharks which pass overhead, and then spit them out after encountering the sharp dorsal spine. The tail, which was tuna-like (symmetrical) externally, was more shark-like internally, with the upper lobe more developed than the lower. The other fins were similar to those of modern sharks, but had much broader attachments to the body at the base, rendering them less flexible, and possibly limiting *Cladoselache's* maneuverability. Those most characteristic of shark appendages – male claspers – are completely lacking in all fossils found to date. Did *Cladoselache* practice external fertilization, unlike all other sharks, or is it just that only female fossils have been found? *Cladoselache* died out around 290 MYA, and is believed not to have contributed to modern lineages – another evolutionary dead end.

The fresh water xenacanthid sharks appear in the fossil record shortly after the appearance of the marine cladodonts. Like *Antarctilamna* and the ctenacanths, they had two-cusped teeth (rather than multi-cusped teeth). Some of the earliest specimens found had already evolved into quite distinctive forms, leading some scientists to speculate that ancestral elasmobranchs must have existed at least 500 MYA. The xenacanths were successful predators which spread around the world and diversified during their 200-MY reign. They vanished about 220 MYA, leaving (as far as we can tell) no descendants.

The latter part of the Paleozoic Era (about 360 to 240 MYA) saw a great many evolutionary experiments among the chondrichthyan fishes.

These juvenile gray reef sharks (Carcharhinus amblyrhynchos) *in Micronesia are also members of the large and highly successful requiem shark family.*

Adaptive radiation of cartilaginous fishes during the Paleozoic Era produced a variety of strange forms. In most cases only teeth, scales, and a few spines or pieces of skeleton have been preserved, leaving artist Ray Troll to guess at the actual body form and color of the animal, in consultation with paleo-ichthyologists. Illustrated are: Helicoprion (top left), a 'scissor-tooth shark'; the eel-like Orthacanthus (top right); Promyxele (bottom left), one of the flying-fish-like iniopterygians; and the frogfish-like Belantsea (bottom right).

Cartilaginous fish dominated the oceans. They comprise 60 per cent of the fossils at some sites, whereas today they account for less than 10 per cent of fish species. The chimaeras, which diverged evolutionarily from the sharks about 400 MYA, diversified and reached their heyday during this period. Since the great extinctions at the end of the Paleozoic, chimaeras have persisted only as a relatively unimportant group of curious fishes which get little respect from scientists, divers, or publishers.

The sharks also diversified into a great many interesting and bizarre forms, most of which left no direct descendants. Some of these strange fossils have only recently been discovered. It is likely that we have found evidence of only a small part of an extremely rich fauna. Rays did not yet exist, although there were some chondrichthyans with flattened bodies. But in addition to the sharks (elasmobranchs) and chimaeras (holocephalans), there were many other chondrichthyans which appear not to belong to either group, and did not leave modern descendants. Some scientists refer to these as 'paraselachians', but, for convenience, we'll call these 'sharks' as well.

Many of the fossils have elaborate ornaments on the head and back, especially in the males. These were likely secondary sexual features – used to attract a mate. They may well have been brightly colored for this same purpose – just as peacocks use their colorful plumage to impress a potential mate. Some of these Paleozoic sharks had already developed the amazing ability to detect electromagnetic fields, a distinctive capability of today's elasmobranchs. Apparently, however, they had not yet developed the ability to project their jaws forward, which is so characteristic of modern sharks. Most had short snouts with the mouth at the end, rather than underneath, so their faces would not have looked very 'shark-like'. In fact, most of the fossil sharks which have been found from the Paleozoic Era were so strange, and so specialized, that scientists cannot imagine that they gave rise to the modern sharks. However, there were undoubtedly many other sharks which were not preserved as fossils. The ancestors of today's sharks may lie among those which are missing from the fossil record. Many of the specialized forms may have died out during the great Permian extinction,

240 MYA, which extinguished up to 95 per cent of life on earth.

Among the most intriguing of these groups are the iniopterygians, small 'sharks' with pectoral fin rays attached close to the back of the head, and elaborate ornamentation on the heads of the males of some species. In some of these, such as *Promyxele* (from about 300 MYA), the pectoral rays are about as long as the rest of the body, and clearly

A male Stethacanthus, *with the mysterious dorsal spine brush.*

supported large wing-like fins. Could these diminutive 4–6 in (10–15 cm) sharks have taken to the air like flying fish to escape the larger sharks which undoubtedly devoured them? Paleontologist Dr Richard Lund, whose team has found many of the fossils, points out that all modern fishes which have the pectoral fins attached so far forward do glide through the air. Other experts doubt that the chunky-bodied fish could have gotten airborne. They suggest that the pectoral fins, which were armored on the front edge with spiny hooks, were merely spread out to increase the apparent size of the fish, in order to deter predators. The tooth plates of *Promyxele* would not have been of much use catching moving prey, so they likely fed on bottom-dwelling shellfish, decreasing the likelihood that they would have migrated to the surface to take flight. The fins may have been used for gliding through the water, to offset negative buoyancy. Or, it is possible they used their 'wings' in the same way as a modern flying gurnard. In spite of the name, gurnards do not fly, but merely spread their brilliantly colored pectoral fins suddenly to startle a predator before swimming away, folding the wings back, and concealing themselves on the bottom.

From what sort of dangers would a little shark need to defend itself with such elaborate structures? The Paleozoic seas abounded with threats. Perhaps the most terrible were the giant scissor-tooth sharks. Fossil tooth whorls, all that remain of *Helicoprion*, baffled paleontologists for years. The teeth are arranged like petals on a spiral with the smallest (first formed) teeth in the center. It is believed that the whorl was lodged within the lower jaw, and the teeth advanced slowly forward, as modern shark teeth move forward to replace the teeth in front. Rather than dropping off, though, as modern shark teeth do, the old teeth of *Helicoprion* remained on the whorl, and were rotated back into the jaw, towards the center of the structure. The teeth were pointed edge-outward (unlike those of all other types of sharks), and may have meshed with matching teeth from the upper jaw to slice up prey like a pair of shears. Spirals have been found up to 28 in (71 cm) across.

If *Helicoprion* was bad, *Edestus* (about 300 MYA) was worse. The tooth rows apparently did not curl around into a whorl as in *Helicoprion*, but stuck straight out like a giant pair of shears. Fossils found to date show only pieces of tooth rows, but one section, with five teeth in it, is 14 in (36 cm) long. How big could the entire 'scissor blade' have been?

Another relative, *Parahelicoprion*, may have been even more formidable. One tooth whorl section (from about 280 MYA) measures 1½ ft (45 cm) across, with teeth over 6 in (15 cm) high. Dr Lund has calculated that the body might have been over 100 ft (30 m) in length – perhaps the largest fish of all time. The sight of it appearing would have been like seeing a giant buzz saw approaching on the front of a locomotive.

Another fierce predator, with sharp multi-cusped teeth, and strong jaws, was the cladodont *Stethacanthus* (about 380 to 300 MYA). This was an open ocean shark, with a high-speed tail, similar to that of a modern mako shark. It grew to about 9 ft (2.75 m). The skin was smooth and scaleless, except for spiny scales on the top of the head and the first dorsal fin which was unlike any structure which has ever existed in any other fish. In fossil impressions, it looks as though the fin has been ripped off and re-attached upside down. The longest part of the fin is the crest, not the base. Furthermore, the crest is covered with spiny denticles, giving it the appearance of a hair brush. The 'spine brush' may be a male secondary sexual feature. Fossils have been found which look like *Stethacanthus*, but without the spine brush and head spines, and without claspers. These could be female *Stethacanthus*. However a fossil has been found which appears to some to be a female with a spine brush. What could the function of this odd structure be? Various explanations have been offered, including defense, courtship, and the idea that it might have been used like a sort of Velcro wand to attach to larger fish passing overhead for a free ride, but nobody really knows the purpose of the mysterious brush.

A counterpart in fresh water was *Orthacanthus*, the 'terror of Permian swamps' (240 to 290 MYA). These giant eel-like xenacanths were the apex predators in estuaries, growing to over 10 ft (3 m), and snapping up prey with massive jaws lined with double-fanged teeth.

Falcatus was a small cladodont, growing to a size of about 1 ft (30 cm). It swam in open water, but was also found in other habitats, about 340 MYA. It fed on shrimp and other small organisms. It may have been a nocturnal hunter, judging by the large eyes. In males, the first dorsal spine curved forward over the head to form an elongated sexual ornament, covered with fine denticles. A pair were fossilized together, with the male's head ornament in the female's mouth. They may have been buried alive, during courtship, by a sudden mudslide.

Even stranger was *Belantsea*, a petalodont, 'petal-toothed', shark (actually more closely related to the chimaeras than to the true sharks) with large blunt, serrated teeth, shaped like artichoke petals. The teeth seem designed for cutting and crushing hard-bodied animals, such as shellfish. The body is lumpy, like a large (up to 3 ft / 90 cm) frogfish, and obviously not designed for speed swimming. *Belantsea* may have

The sleek, efficient, torpedo-like shape of some present-day sharks, such as this silky shark (Carcharhinus falciformis), is not a feature which achieved perfection 400 million years ago, but rather one of many body forms adopted by modern sharks over a long period of evolutionary experimentation.

Eagle rays (Aetobatus narinari) are among the most recently evolved of the batoid elasmobranchs, or 'pancake sharks'. The eagle ray family has been around for less than 60 million years. They evolved from bottom-dwelling rays, and continue to feed on the bottom, but 'fly' in open water when not feeding.

crawled about the bottom on its fins, grubbing for clams. It may have been brightly colored to blend in with sponges or other bottom fauna. It lived in the shallow seas covering North America about 340 MYA.

An assemblage of sharks which may contain the ancestors of today's sharks begins to show up in the fossil record about 320 MYA, shortly after the extinction of the armored placoderm fishes. These were the hybodont sharks, which had sharp multi-cusped teeth in front, for cutting, and flat teeth at the back, for crushing. This permitted them to exploit a variety of food sources, including both fish and shellfish. Some were clearly bottom feeders. Their fins were narrow at the base, like those of modern sharks, enabling them to turn the fins to maneuver while swimming. This gave them a distinct advantage over the stiff-finned cladodonts. They also had an anal fin (unpaired fin behind the pelvic fins), which is present in most modern sharks, but lacking in cladodonts. Males had claspers (curiously absent in all specimens of *Cladoselache* found to date). They also had a set of small 'antlers' or 'horns' on the sides of the head (properly known as 'cephalic spines'). It is interesting to speculate how these might have been used in attracting, competing for, or subduing mates. Some also had sharp spines in the front of the dorsal fins, like modern horn sharks.

Some of the hybodonts retained the ancestral simple form of jaw suspension, but others developed the form found in most modern sharks, which permits the jaws to distend and open much wider than would otherwise be possible. The combination of internal fertilization, which enables better protection for the developing egg, and a huge jaw gape, which must have increased predatory success, seems to have been a winner. The hybodonts spread over the entire world, occupying both marine and fresh water habitats. They persisted until the beginning of the Cenozoic (modern) Era, about 65 MYA, disappearing at about the same time as the dinosaurs.

The first 'modern' sharks, or neoselachians, begin to show up in the fossil record about 200 MYA. They may have evolved from hybodonts, or may be a 'sister group', descended from a common ancestor. The earliest known neoselachian was a skinny little thing (less than 3 ft /

90 cm long) called *Paleospinax*. The most notable characteristic of this shark was a sectioned backbone composed of calcified vertebrae. Up until this time, sharks had a continuous boneless structure called a notochord, but all subsequent elasmobranchs have had the spinal chord sheathed in hard vertebrae. The most ancient fossils of batoid or ray-like elasmobranchs also date from about this time, although the

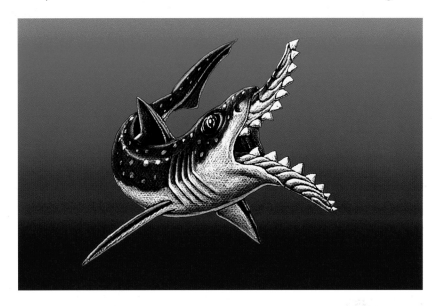

Edestus giganteus may have looked like giant swimming kitchen shears.

first stingrays did not appear until about 60 MYA. Saw sharks, guitarfishes, and electric rays are believed to have been the first batoids to evolve. Mantas, stingrays, and eagle rays are the most recent.

Among the earliest of the modern shark families to appear were the cow sharks (including six-gill and seven-gill sharks), cat sharks, and horn sharks. By 100 MYA, the first wobbegongs, sand tigers, dogfish, thresher, and mackerel sharks had appeared. Soon, large mako-like sharks were attacking even giant swimming reptiles. Modern-looking rays, skates, and sawfishes had become common.

About 65 MYA, the earth went through a major upheaval. Sudden climatic changes precipitated a wave of extinctions. The dinosaurs disappeared, and so did their gigantic aquatic relatives – the ichthyosaurs, mososaurs, and plesiosaurs. The only large swimming reptiles to survive were the crocodilians, which are primarily fresh water and estuarine, and sea turtles, which feed on plants and slow-moving invertebrates. Competition for the large aquatic predator niche was greatly reduced. Shortly afterwards, mammals began to colonize aquatic habitats, evolving into the first cetaceans (whales and dolphins). This added new competitors and new predators on the smaller elasmobranchs, but it also created a new food source for the larger elasmobranchs. Freed from the limitations of gravity, marine mammals evolved into larger and larger forms. And the sharks which preyed upon them grew larger and larger to take advantage of the new resource.

Great white sharks first appeared on earth around 60 MYA, evolving from an ancestral mackerel shark, which also gave rise to the mako sharks. Only one species survives today, but at least seven are known from the fossil record. One of these, *Carcharodon* (or *Carcharocles*) *megalodon*, the 'megatooth shark', was one of the largest predators ever to stalk the planet. *Tyrannosaurus rex*, if it had survived, would have seemed puny by comparison. The actual length attained by megatooth can only be surmised by the size of the teeth it left behind, but experts believe it reached about 50–60 ft (15–18 m). This is larger than most whales. Whale skeletons which occur in fossil deposits along with *megalodon* teeth have bite marks which can only have come from these teeth. Fossilized *megalodon* teeth, which occur in large numbers, can be truly impressive, reaching a height of 6¾ in (17 cm). Modern white shark teeth reach a height of 'only' 2¼ in (6 cm).

Interestingly, the preserved teeth seem to become larger as the fossil history of megatooth progresses. The earliest known white shark, *Carcharodon orientalis*, about 60 MYA, had teeth about the same size as today's white shark. Species that existed from 55 to 24 MYA had teeth up to 5 in (13 cm) in height. *Carcharodon megalodon* first appears in the fossil record about 15 to 20 MYA, but the largest teeth found are only 2 to 10 million years old. This size progression may correspond with

the increasing size of the marine mammals that white sharks preyed upon. It appears that juvenile *megalodon* fed on the smaller-toothed whales, while adults fed on the larger baleen whales. Inexplicably, megatooth vanished from the oceans around 2 MYA. Its demise may have had to do with the extinction of the cetotheres, small baleen whales that were an important part of its diet. The modern baleen whales that replaced them undertake extensive migrations, spending a large part of every year in high latitudes where they may have been unavailable to *megalodon* due to the cold water temperatures.

By the time megatooth became extinct, it was already sharing the seas with *Carcharodon carcharias*, the modern white shark. This species first appeared 4 to 10 MYA. It may be derived directly from megatooth, but is more likely descended from a common ancestor. Why *C. carcharias* was able to outlive its large-toothed cousin is not known, but it may have to do with changing water temperatures. When white sharks first appeared, the seas were warm all over the planet. As the oceans began to cool at higher latitudes, warm-blooded marine mammals favored the more temperate regions. The modern white shark has a blood vessel heat exchange system which enables it to maintain some parts of its body at a temperature higher than the surrounding sea water – probably a critical factor in being able to hunt successfully in temperate waters. It is not known whether megatooth had this capability or not. The modern white shark also specializes in feeding on seals and sea lions, most of which do not undertake migrations as extensive as baleen whales, which were the favored diet of *megalodon*.

The first tiger sharks (*Galeocerdo*) appear in the fossil record not long after white sharks, about 56 MYA, followed by lemon sharks (*Negaprion*) and reef sharks (*Carcharhinus*) about 42 MYA. The most recent shark family to appear is the hammerheads (*Sphyrnidae*), with the first occurrence about 24 MYA, and some types known only from the last 5 MY. Of course, the fossil record is incomplete. New discoveries may require us to revise our estimates of when certain animals first evolved.

Hammerheads are the most recent shark family to evolve. Great white sharks appeared earlier, but the modern species (p.30) is less than 10 MY old.

Living in the Sea

Living in a medium which is 800 times denser than air, elasmobranchs have had to adapt to an environment that is very dissimilar to the environment in which we live.

Water poses a much greater resistance to movement than air, but also provides the possibility of movement in three dimensions, if an animal can achieve something close to neutral buoyancy and float without sinking or being ballooned up to the surface. This was easy enough for primitive invertebrates, whose bodies were mostly water anyway, but the first vertebrates – fish – had to find a way to support the weight of a skeleton and other tissues that were considerably denser than water.

Most bony fish accomplish this by means of a swim bladder which holds air or other gases. This has the advantage that buoyancy can be precisely adjusted at any depth by adding or removing gas from the swim bladder. It has the disadvantage that this can only be done at a certain rate, limiting the speed with which the fish can safely change depth. Fish that ascend more rapidly than they can absorb the gases in their swim bladder (for example when being pulled to the surface by a fisher) suffer a rapid expansion of the bladder with extremely unpleasant results.

A preferred hunting strategy of the great white, and some other species of sharks, is to stalk prey from below, then make a sudden rush upwards to seize it. They are able to utilize this feeding method without risk of explosion because elasmobranchs took a whole different approach to the problem of buoyancy control. Only gases change their volume significantly with changes in pressure, so if no gas is used for buoyancy control, the 'exploding fish syndrome' is avoided.

The buoyancy advantage may have been a critical factor in the evolutionary 'choice' of cartilage as the skeletal material. Cartilage is only slightly more dense than water. Bone is twice as dense as water. Oil, on the other hand, is less dense than water. For this reason, many sharks have large livers that contain high amounts of oil. The livers of blue sharks, for example, may contribute up to 20 per cent of the total body weight. The oil provides an energy reserve, but is also crucial in maintaining neutral buoyancy.

Some sharks, especially deep-sea sharks, have sufficient liver oil to attain neutral buoyancy. But most are still denser than sea water. For some sharks, and most rays, this is not a problem. They merely spend most of their time resting on the bottom. Most sharks, however, counteract their negative buoyancy with lift achieved by swimming through the water. The pectoral and tail fins of most sharks are shaped like airplane wings. Water flowing across the curved surface is accelerated, resulting in a reduced pressure, which creates lift. In some sharks, notably hammerheads, the head is also shaped like a hydrodynamic foil, and probably also creates lift.

One type of shark has devised a unique behavioral solution to the buoyancy problem. Sand tigers are known to swim to the surface and gulp air. They retain the air in the stomach, enabling it to serve as a swim bladder. The bubble of swallowed air enables sand tigers to hover almost motionless, without expending energy in swimming, as most sharks must.

Sand tigers are the only elasmobranchs known to go to the surface for air. All sharks and rays, however, require oxygen. Like all fishes, they extract it from sea water by means of delicate organs called gills. Sharks and rays have 5–7 gill slits on each side of the head, for water to leave the body after passing over the gills. Bony fishes and chimaeras have only a single gill opening. In most sharks, water is passed over the gills by opening the mouth while swimming. The nostrils are dead ends, used only for smelling, and not connected to the respiratory passageways. In some bottom-dwelling sharks, water can be pumped in through the first gill slit, then out through the others.

Rays have all of their gill slits on the underside of their bodies. They pump their breathing water in through a large opening called a spiracle, which is just behind the eye. The spiracle is derived from the first gill opening, but has been evolutionarily modified to become an intake valve. Some types of sharks also have spiracles. Bottom-dwelling species use them like rays to draw in water for respiration, but in other species it is not known what function they serve, if any.

The gills are essential to the survival of a shark. So are the mouth, the nostrils, the eyes, and the cloaca (genital and waste disposal opening). Yet all of these openings in the skin expose the shark to a deadly threat: the water in which it lives. To survive, every animal must maintain an internal environment that is different from the external environment surrounding it. All vertebrates have blood which is saltier than fresh water, but less salty than sea water. To maintain this differential, an aquatic animal must fight the power of osmosis. Osmosis is the diffusion of water across a semi-permeable barrier, such as a membrane, which separates a fish's bloodstream from the water in which it swims. Skin provides an impermeable barrier that prevents osmosis, but membranes such as those lining the mouth, gills, etc. allow the passage of both water and various ions. Water moves from the weaker to the stronger solution until the concentrations are the same on both sides of the barrier.

In the case of fresh-water fish, body fluids are more concentrated than the water around them, so water tends to move into the fish's body, causing bloating, and dilution of the blood, unless it is expelled as urine. Marine fish have the opposite problem. Osmosis draws water from the fish to the sea, dehydrating the fish. Bony sea fish counteract osmosis by drinking sea water, and excreting the excess salt ions.

But elasmobranchs have a completely different solution to the problem. Instead of replacing the water lost by osmosis, they prevent its loss by maintaining body fluids at a concentration equal to or higher than that of sea water. To have as much salt as sea water in the blood would be as deadly for a shark as it would be for us. But elasmobranchs do not concentrate their blood with salt. They do it with nitrogen compounds, including urea and related metabolic products. For this reason, shark flesh is considered poor-quality food by many people. But it can be cleansed of these products by soaking before preparation.

The total concentration of salts, urea, and similar compounds in the blood of elasmobranchs is actually slightly higher than in sea water. Therefore, instead of water diffusing out of their bodies, it diffuses slowly inwards, eliminating the need to drink. However, water is not the only problem. If a membrane is permeable to salt ions (sodium and chloride), then they will likewise pass from the solution where they are more concentrated (sea water) to the one where they are less concentrated (body fluids). Salt water is also taken in incidentally during feeding. Elasmobranchs rid their bodies of excess salt primarily by excreting ions through a special gland, called the rectal gland, located in the cloaca. Some salt ions are also forced out through the gills. Rectal glands are found only in elasmobranchs and in the coelacanth. Other bony fishes excrete salt ions only through their gills.

Fresh water sharks and rays deal with their water and salt balance problems in essentially the same way as other fresh-water fish. Excess water which enters the body through osmosis is excreted as copious amounts of very weak urine (up to a third of the body weight per day). Salts are replaced through the diet and pumped inward, rather than outward, at the gills. Since fresh-water elasmobranchs have no need of a rectal gland, it is much smaller than in marine species. And urea is retained in much smaller amounts, or not at all.

Heat transfer occurs about twenty times faster in water than in air, so it is much more difficult for aquatic animals to maintain an elevated body temperature than it is for terrestrial animals. Most don't. Like other fish, most sharks are 'cold-blooded' – their body temperatures vary with the temperature of the surrounding water. Although the majority of sharks inhabit tropical to subtropical waters, there are many which live in cooler waters, even in the near-freezing waters of the deep sea and under the Arctic ice. In general, each species is adapted to a certain temperature range, and will avoid water that is warmer or

Sand tiger sharks (Carcharias taurus) *are unique in achieving neutral buoyancy by swallowing air and using their stomachs as flotation chambers.*

cooler than its preferred range. However, some kinds of sharks can tolerate a wide range of temperatures. Great white sharks are known to roam from the tropics to cool temperate waters. In recent years, scientists have discovered that white sharks, and the closely related mako and porbeagle sharks (together known as mackerel sharks), are able to maintain body temperatures up to at least 25°F (14°C) above the ambient water temperature. In fact, there is mounting evidence that they may be truly 'warm-blooded', that is, able to maintain a constant body temperature regardless of changing water temperature.

White sharks keep their muscle tissue, their stomachs, their brains, and their eyes warmer than the water in which they swim. All of these organs function more efficiently at higher temperatures, enabling them to be more proficient hunters. They control heat loss by means of a counter-current exchange system. Veins returning blood from muscles where it has been heated by muscular activity lie next to arteries bringing in cooler blood flowing in the opposite direction. Heat is transferred from the returning veinous blood to the incoming arterial blood, and is retained within the tissues instead of being lost to the water when the blood flows back to the gills for oxygenation.

Warmer bodies give these mackerel sharks an enormous advantage in hunting their prey, some of which, such as tuna and seals, are also warm-blooded. Mako sharks may be the fastest-swimming fish in the ocean. They have to be, in order to catch the very quick mackerels and tuna which form a large part of their diet. Digestion improves at higher temperatures, too, as a result of the increased activity of digestive enzymes. Bluefin tuna have been shown to be able to increase their food-processing capacity by a factor of three due to their elevated gut temperature. Perhaps more importantly, higher body temperatures enable these sharks to enter cooler water than they could otherwise tolerate, to take advantage of food resources there. Adult white sharks show a preference for feeding on marine mammals, such as seals and sea lions, which favor cooler waters.

Counter-current heat exchange vessels have also been found around the brains of manta rays, and two species of mobula (devil) rays. The mobulas also appear to have the equipment to warm their guts, and in one case the body musculature as well. Mantas and mobulas feed on plankton which tends to collect in dense layers at the ocean surface and in a much deeper zone, known as the 'deep scattering layer'. Water temperature can vary greatly between these two zones. It is possible that warming the brain keeps the nervous system from going into shock from rapid temperature change, and permits mantas and devil rays to exploit both food sources. It could also make it easier for them to exploit plankton blooms that occur in areas where upwellings bring cold nutrient-rich water to the surface.

Warmed swimming muscles give makos an increase in power, but cannot alone explain their phenomenal speed, which exceeds theoretical predictions of how fast an object can move through a dense medium such as sea water. The secret seems to be in the dermal denticles, which channel water flow, and prevent the build-up of turbulence. Aircraft engineers are experimenting with grooves called riblets, which work in the same way to reduce turbulence. The U.S. entry in the 1987 America's Cup sailing race had a riblet hull coating. After it won the race, such designs were banned from the competition. Engineers predict that a 10 per cent reduction in drag can be achieved with riblets, but sharks seem to exceed this. Some scientists have noted that shark denticles are attached to subskin muscles, and have suggested that the denticles might be adjusted during swimming to reduce drag.

Dolphins have a spongy skin which acts as a 'compliant surface' to reduce drag, but neither they nor any other animals have anything like the turbulence-baffling denticles on the skin of elasmobranchs. These, and many other features, including highly effective sensory capabilities (to be discussed in the next chapter), are found only in sharks and their allies. Sharks may indeed be considered 'primitive' in the sense of having a long and distinguished ancestry, and retaining some anatomic characters from those earliest ancestors. But they can also aptly be described as 'technologically advanced' in terms of possessing many specialized adaptations which are unique to this amazing and extremely successful group of animals.

Manta rays (Manta birostris) have recently been discovered to have a counter-current heat exchange system in the blood vessels surrounding the brain. This may prevent thermal shock when the animal dives into cold water at depth.

*The two barbels hanging from the upper 'lip' of this nurse shark (*Ginglymostoma cirratum*) are taste organs used to probe for food in bottom sediments.*

Data Input

Sharks are often described as 'swimming noses'. For many elasmobranchs, the sense of smell is vitally important for finding food, and may also be used in social activities, such as finding a mating partner, for navigation, and for other purposes. This is reflected in the large size of the olfactory bulbs and the forebrain, which is devoted primarily to smell. However, this part of the brain also processes some visual, electro-sensory, and mechano-sensory information, indicating that the senses of sharks, as in other animals, work in an integrated fashion. Lemon sharks, when captured and released several miles away from their home range, will orient themselves and swim back to the capture location. They do this even with their eyes covered, their nostrils blocked, or their electrosense disrupted with magnets. Obviously they do not depend upon just a single sense for navigation.

The ability of sharks to home in on an odor source is legendary. Some types of sharks are able to detect fish extracts in water at concentrations lower than one part in 10 billion, and can follow an odor corridor for miles to reach a dead or injured fish. Oceanic whitetip sharks may be able to extend their olfactory range even further by lifting their snouts out of the water and 'sniffing' the air.

For species with different feeding strategies, the sense of smell may be less important, and consequently less developed. Angel sharks are primarily visual predators which lie on the bottom and snap at anything of the right size that passes overhead. Even for sharks which rely heavily on smell to lead them to dead or wounded fish, the sense of smell may not be the longest range sense. The sounds emitted by struggling wounded fish can draw in sharks from even greater distances.

Smell is what scientists refer to as a 'chemosensory' faculty, the ability to detect dissolved molecules of various substances. Water bearing the molecules enters the nares, or nostrils, on the snout, and the molecules bind to special receptor cells inside, which send a signal to the brain. The passage of water through the nares is most often accomplished by swimming, but sedentary species are able to pump water across their nares in order to sample it.

Taste is also a chemosensory function, and works in essentially the same way as smell. Taste receptors, however, send messages to a different part of the brain than do smell receptors. They are also located on a different surface of the body, typically on taste buds inside the mouth. Barbels — whisker-like appendages dangling from the upper 'lip' of some species, such as nurse sharks — are probably taste organs. These bottom feeders apparently use them to detect food buried in the sand. Taste typically functions at very close range — usually upon contact with a food item — and is less sensitive than smell. Nevertheless, taste is an important sense, and probably plays a crucial role in determining whether a shark swallows or rejects a food item. In over half of reported attacks on humans by great white sharks, the victim received only a single bite. It has been suggested (among other theories), that this is because the shark finds the human unpalatable, either because of a neoprene wet suit, fiberglass surfboard or other contaminant, or because of a low fat content compared with tuna, elephant seals, and sea lions — the white shark's normal prey.

Few aquatic animals have external ears. These can create drag and noise moving through the water, and are unnecessary since sound travels faster and farther through water than air. Most sea animals hear quite well without them, and sharks are no exception. Tiny openings on top of the head lead through canals to the inner ear, where sound signals are received by hair cells. The sound vibration deflects the hair, which sends a nerve signal to the brain, in a similar manner to a phonograph needle, or computer joystick. Sharks are particularly sensitive to low-frequency sounds, and can be attracted from miles away to speakers broadcasting irregularly pulsed, low-frequency sounds. Such sounds mimic the vibrations given off by struggling injured fish.

In spite of their excellent hearing, no elasmobranchs are known to deliberately produce sounds. Communication between members of a species seems to be primarily by scents and body language.

The inner ear also contains (like ours) three semicircular canals at right angles to each other. Any turning motions by the shark cause the fluid to move within the canal which is oriented to that plane of movement. The moving fluid deflects the hairs in the sensors, and gives the shark feedback about its movements. Below the semicircular canals are three otolith organs. These contain sand-like particles that press on hair cells according to the force of gravity, or acceleration. The hair cells are arranged in a different plane in each otolith organ, so that the combined input gives a three-dimensional sensation. Together, these systems give the shark a very precise sense of balance, orientation, and movement.

Hair cells very similar to the ones in the inner ear are also found on the outside of sharks' bodies. These occur both in individual pit organs, and in rows within canals that branch across the shark's head and run along the side of the body and the upper lobe of the tail. These canals constitute the lateral line system, which is also present in bony fish. The lateral line and pit organ sensors are known as 'mechanoreceptors'. The hair cells within them send signals to the brain when the hairs are deflected by water displacement waves. Moving objects in water create both compression waves, or sound, and displacement waves. The displacement wave is the actual disturbance, or movement of water, and is sensed at much closer range than sound. Even so, it probably enables a shark to detect a moving object at some distance from its own body. At close range, even stationary objects may be detected by sensing water that reflects off them after being set in motion by waves, currents, the shark's own movement, or any other disturbance. The mechanoreceptors can also directly detect currents and other water movements important for orientation and navigation.

In stingrays the lateral line system extends over both the upper and lower surfaces of the body. It is supposed that the upper body receptors serve primarily to warn of predators, whereas those on the underside function in prey detection. The tail is covered with pit organs, presumably to warn of attacks by predatory sharks.

Some parts of the lateral line system, especially on the underside of the head, do not have openings to the outside. Therefore the hair cells within are not very sensitive to water movements. These are believed to function as touch receptors, primarily for use in handling prey.

Additionally, there are nerve endings at different depths within the skin and other tissues which sense touch, temperature, and stretching of muscles or other tissues. These provide feedback about the animal's position and movements as well as information about external stimuli. Mechanoreceptors in the skin send out signals when the skin is depressed as little as 0.0008 in (0.02 mm).

Most elasmobranchs have relatively large, well-developed eyes, suggesting that vision is an important sense for this group of animals. Some are primarily visual predators, whereas most rely on a whole battery of senses to find and capture prey. In some, such as stingrays, which feed on quarry buried in the sand beneath them, vision may be of little help in feeding, but is nonetheless consequential in avoiding predation and in other activities. Torpedo (electric) rays have the smallest elasmobranch eyes. The largest, at up to 5 in (12.5 cm) in diameter, belong to the big-eye thresher. Its huge eyes wrap around onto the top of its head, enabling it to look straight up at the schooling fish it feeds on.

The wide-set eyes of sharks, combined with swinging of the head during swimming, give them nearly panoramic vision of their surroundings. At the same time, there is an overlap in front where they have binocular vision, enabling them to judge the distance of prey or hazards ahead. Rays tend to have both eyes on top of the body, and depend on other senses to detect what is beneath them.

At least 20 species of sharks have been found to have both cones (for color vision) and rods (for high-sensitivity black and white vision) in their retinas. The sixgill shark, which normally lives in deep water where light is dim and colors don't penetrate, has only rods. Other deep-sea

*Like a cat's eye, the pupil in the eye of this blacktip shark (Carcharhinus limbatus)
contracts to a vertical slit in bright light. The eyes of other elasmobranchs have pupils
which contract to round or U-shaped openings in bright light. Also like a cat, this shark has
a reflective layer in the back of the eye which can double the amount of light hitting
the retina. Contrary to popular opinion, most sharks do NOT have poor vision.*

Young lemon sharks (Negaprion brevirostris) *live in shallow estuarine environments, where the full spectrum of color is visible. Therefore it is not surprising that they appear to have the ability to sense various colors of light. Deep-water sharks may respond mostly to light at the blue end of the spectrum.*

sharks may lack color vision as well, and some that do see color are most sensitive to blue light. Likewise, open ocean sharks could be expected to show the greatest sensitivity in the blue and green spectra, as do other open ocean fish. The lemon shark, a shallow lagoon and reef species, responded to red and other colors of light in experiments, but it has not been shown conclusively if any elasmobranchs distinguish between different colors, apart from responding to brightness. Both experimental evidence and analysis of shark attacks indicate that sharks may be more likely to bite at dark objects or light-colored objects, depending upon their normal type of prey and hunting methods. Great white shark attacks are disproportionately directed towards black-clothed victims, which is not surprising, because white sharks hunt dark-bodied seals by spotting a dark silhouette when looking up towards the bright sky. Fish-eating sharks, by contrast, seem to favor yellow or white, colors that contrast with the dark background of water much like the light silvery shades of small fish.

Like humans, elasmobranchs adjust their eyes to lowered light levels for 'night vision'. Most elasmobranchs can dilate their pupils to admit more light, an ability which is shared by mammals, but lacking in most other fishes. The retina can also adjust to dimmer light. The light sensitivity of lemon sharks increases a million-fold after an hour in the dark. Most elasmobranchs have a reflective layer behind the retina called the tapetum lucidum. The tapetum is formed of mirror-like mineral crystals which reflect incoming light back onto the photoreceptors in the retina, effectively doubling their sensitivity. Cats, alligators, and other nocturnal animals have a similar adaptation, which is responsible for the 'eye shine' that reflects from their eyes under a spotlight. The tapetum in sharks is twice as efficient as that in cats. It reflects back up to 90 per cent of incoming light, creating an eyeshine which varies from blue-green to gold. Lemon sharks respond to light at a level only 10 per cent of the threshold for humans, and some sharks are probably much more sensitive. Some experts believe they are able to hunt by starlight.

In bright light, sharks are able to cover their tapetum to avoid reflecting excess light onto the retina, an ability that is lacking in cats

and other animals. Most sharks can also contract their pupils to limit the amount of light entering the eye, although some, such as sixgill sharks, cannot, and must avoid bright light. In many sharks, the pupil constricts to a slit, as it does in cats. However, in some skates and rays, the pupil constricts to a crescent shape in bright light. A similar shape is found in some fishes and mammals. This shape increases the size of the visual field and reduces spherical aberration (distortion). Tests with a camera fitted with an opening of this shape reveal that depth of field (the distance range over which objects are seen in sharp focus) is reduced from what it would be with a round opening. Out-of-focus points of light appear in a U-shape. Furthermore, the U is either right side up, or upside down, depending upon whether the reflecting point is in front of, or behind, the plane of focus. What this means is that there is an effective range-finding mechanism in the eye. The amount and direction of adjustment required to bring an object into focus would measure the distance to that object. This implies that rays can measure distance with a single eye, and do not require binocular vision for depth perception, as we do. This is important because they have binocular vision in only a small part of their visual field.

Some sharks and rays have another odd structure – a sort of fringed eye shade that lowers over the pupil to control the amount of light entering. Interestingly, the 'shade' is divided into flaps which form multiple openings for light to enter the eye. Recent tests have shown that this structure produces results very similar to a crescent-shaped pupil. Having more than one opening for light to enter the eye increases the size of the visual field, reduces spherical aberration, and reduces depth of field. Out-of-focus objects produce multiple images that merge as focus is achieved, just as they do in old-fashioned range-finder cameras. Multiple pupil openings also occur in some dolphins, llamas, horses, and geckos (which need very precise distance ranging to target their insect prey). Multiple pupil openings are most likely to be found in species which are primarily active at night, but also require effective vision under conditions of very bright light. Nocturnal animals typically lack a fovea (the cone-rich part of the retina where light is

focused for binocular vision), and this mechanism apparently allows them to achieve distance-ranging capability without one.

Most sharks have small 'lids' above and below the eye that are unable to cover it. Additionally, requiem sharks and some others have a 'third eyelid' or nictitating membrane that comes up from below to protect the eye. This is used during feeding and similar situations to protect against physical injury. Mackerel sharks, such as makos and great whites, do not have a nictitating membrane, but instead are able to roll the eyeball completely around into the head for protection, exposing only a tough layer on the back of the eyeball.

Some sharks also sense light that is transmitted through a thin area in the top of the skull to the pineal gland in the brain. This structure has no lens to focus the light, and therefore cannot form an image, but it is very sensitive, and can respond to changes in light levels which are below the level of moonlight at the water's surface. This may be used to help the shark regulate its activity cycles. Deep-sea sharks may use this structure to guide their migrations up and down in the water column.

In addition to the familiar senses, chondrichthyans have a 'sixth sense', which is shared only with a few other types of fish. Their electrosense gives them remarkable capabilities that may play a large part in explaining why they have been such a successful group over a long period of evolutionary history. The electrosense organs are known as 'ampullae of Lorenzini', and consist of small pouches beneath the skin, lined with hair cells and connected to an opening on the skin via a tube filled with conductive jelly. The ampullae are concentrated on the head and lower jaw. The organs are clustered together in groups, but their tubes spread outward to separate pores on the skin so that each cluster can compare voltage potentials between different locations. With this apparatus, sharks and rays can detect electric fields as slight as 5 billionths of a volt per cm. This is equivalent to the electric field that would be generated by a flashlight battery if the two poles were 2000 miles (3200 km) apart.

What would a fish do with such an extraordinary capability? The possibilities include finding and taking prey, locating mates, orientation and navigation, and social communication, as well as other uses we can't even imagine. All animals generate a weak electric field around their bodies as a result of electric activity in the muscles, which are in a state of constant partial contraction, even when not in use. In water, the electric 'aura' is stronger, and is primarily due to ions leaking in and out of the animal's body through various membranes such as the gills, eyes, mouth, spiracle, cloaca, etc. If the animal's skin is cut or punctured, the ionic trickle becomes a flood, and the electric field increases greatly in strength.

Sharks and rays take advantage of this electric field to locate prey buried beneath the sand. For stingrays, this could include clams, shrimp, worms, and sea stars. For sharks the buried prey could include stingrays and skates, as well as fish such as wrasses. One proposed explanation of the wide lobes on the heads of hammerhead sharks is that they enlarge and extend the receptor area for the electrosense. Stingrays are a favorite food of great hammerhead sharks, while scalloped hammerheads are known to feed on buried fish. Sightings of hammerheads swinging their heads just above the surface of the sand, as if using a metal detector, give credence to this theory. Skates typically respond to a threat by freezing in position, suspending ventilation, and closing the spiracle. This strategy minimizes the electric field both by reducing muscular activity and by blocking ionic flow at the spiracle, and may help the skate to avoid detection by a prowling shark.

Electro-detection is also used for capture of prey previously targeted by sight or other senses. In the final stage of an attack, a shark typically covers or rolls back its eye to avoid injury by the struggling prey animal. The electrosense is used to guide its jaws to the target. This explains why sharks attracted to bait will often switch and bite a shark cage, boat propeller, or swim platform at the last moment. Once the eyes are closed, the electrosense guides the shark to the strongest

This pelagic stingray (Dasyatis violacea) is obviously using senses other than sight to feed upon squid in a mating aggregation at night.

electric field – in this case the galvanic discharge of metal in sea water. In the laboratory, sharks and rays given a choice between an electrode and a tube discharging fish juices consistently bit the electrode.

The electrosense also provides an explanation for why sharks may continue to attack a wounded person while ignoring rescuers and other persons in the water. Each injury increases the magnitude of the victim's electric field, and leads the shark back to the most vulnerable prey.

It has been proposed that sharks hunting in open water may use a shifting hierarchy of senses during an attack. They may be first alerted to an injured fish by hearing its erratic tail beats. Approaching the direction of the sound, they may pick up the scent trail of its blood and juices, and follow that to within visual range. By the time they can see their prey, they will also be able to pick up any disturbance it is making in the water by means of the lateral line. They may bump the prey to get some tactile input. When the decision is made to sample the item, the eyes are closed, and control is switched to the electrosense. Then the senses of taste and touch take over to make the final decision whether to feed or not.

Stingrays use their electrosense to find mates as well as prey. During the mating season males may be attracted to the vicinity of ovulating females by pheromones or scent signals, but if the females are buried in the sand, it is the electrosense that enables the males to locate them. Skates use their electrosense to detect electric discharges given off by other skates, which may help them locate a suitable mate, assess a potential partner's receptivity, identify the species of a nearby skate, avoid territorial conflicts, or serve in some other form of social communication.

The earth's magnetic field may also provide a source of vital information via the 'sixth sense'. Some birds, whales, and sea turtles have been found to contain magnetite in their heads, which would enable them to navigate by use of a built-in compass. Magnetite has not been found in elasmobranchs, but they can likely use the earth's field anyway, due to the close relationship between magnetism and electricity. Any charged particle that moves through a magnetic field creates an electric field. This includes the sodium and chloride ions that make up most of the salt in sea water. Therefore an ocean current creates an electric field as it flows through the earth's magnetic field. By sensing the field generated by a current, a shark can obtain information about its position with respect to that current, and also about the state of tides and other factors that affect current flow. Since a shark's body also contains ions, it will generate an electric field as it swims through the earth's magnetic field. By sensing fluctuations in its own electric field, the shark can measure small differences in the earth's magnetism, caused by magnetic rocks on the sea floor. These magnetic anomalies can be read as a map, and used very effectively to navigate across the open ocean where there are no other clues. This may help to explain how highly migratory sharks such as blue sharks find their way all the way across ocean basins.

Some elasmobranchs can generate, as well as detect, electric potentials. This ability features in the torpedo rays, which can discharge up to 220 volts, enough to give a human a serious shock, or possibly even knock a person unconscious. Torpedo rays use this weapon both for defense and for stunning prey. Presumably, they have some way to prevent their own discharges from interfering with their electrosense. Skates, which produce a much weaker discharge (2 volts or less), only discharge when they are near other skates, not when they are alone. They can perceive the discharges of other skates, but apparently not their own, leading researchers to the conclusion that the 'shock signals' are used for communication with other members of the species. Some researchers believe that the primary function of electric organs in skates is to enable them to recognize a suitable mate. This theory is supported by observations that skates in mating aggregations discharge their electric organs frequently. Others have suggested that a skate's discharge could be used to confuse or surprise a shark (the main enemies of skates) by suddenly stimulating its electrosense, enabling the skate to escape, even though the shock might not be strong enough to disable a predator.

This southern stingray (Dasyatis americana) has buried itself in the sand to conceal itself from predators. However, it is still vulnerable to sharks, especially great hammerheads, which swim low over the bottom, swinging their broad heads to search for the electric fields generated by living organisms.

Counting Calories

Although obesity can be a problem for sharks held in captivity, elasmobranchs in the wild are primarily concerned with obtaining enough calories to fuel their needs for daily metabolism, growth, and reproduction. Starvation is a constant threat for most wild animals. Any way that an animal can reduce its food requirements will enhance its chances of survival. In stark contrast to their popular image as 'feeding machines', most sharks and rays have adopted an energy conservation lifestyle that enables them to survive for moderate to very long periods without feeding, so that they can take advantage of spotty food resources when they become available. The metabolic rate and digestive rate of elasmobranchs are generally lower than for other fishes, and much less than for mammals. Bottom-dwelling species tend to lie quietly on the sea floor when not feeding, expending very little energy. Pelagic species tend to glide on outstretched pectoral fins, consuming a minimum of calories when not actively pursuing prey or mates. All elasmobranchs have a unique structure called an intestinal valve in the digestive system. In some groups this takes the form of a spiral valve, while other groups have a ring valve. The intestinal valve substantially increases the surface area of the intestine for food absorption, so that a long intestine is not needed. At the same time, it greatly slows the passage of food through the intestine.

Even the shortfin mako, an active, fast-swimming, warm-blooded shark, takes 1½ to 2 days to digest an average-sized meal, and consumes food equal to about 3 per cent of its body weight per day. Sandbar, blue, and lemon sharks take 3 to 4 days to digest a meal. And the nurse shark, a more sedentary species, eats only 0.2–0.3 per cent of its body weight per day, and takes six days or more to digest a meal. Some experts believe that great white sharks may go a month or longer between meals. And basking sharks shed their feeding structures (the gill rakers used to filter plankton from the water) each fall, and then vanish for the winter. When they reappear in spring, they regrow their feeding apparatus. It is possible that they hibernate on the bottom without feeding for several months. By contrast, dolphins eat 4–12 per cent of their body weight per day and some fish eat up to 30 per cent of their body weight per day. Dolphins and some of the bony fishes are absolutely voracious in comparison to sharks.

All elasmobranchs depend upon animal protein for sustenance. None are able to extract energy from the sun by photosynthesis, and none feed to any significant degree upon plants. So all are mid to higher order carnivores. Some feed on tiny zooplankton, and some on benthic invertebrates, such as clams, crabs, and shrimp. At least one (the cookie cutter shark) has adopted what could be termed a parasitic lifestyle, removing pieces of flesh from much larger victims which are not killed in the process.

Some sharks have extremely specialized diets. For example, 97 per cent of the diet of the starry smoothhound is crustaceans. Other elasmobranchs are generalized predators, feeding on a wide variety of fish and invertebrates. Many sharks feed primarily on fish (including other elasmobranchs) and squid. A few species also consume sea turtles, sea snakes, birds, and marine mammals. The larger predatory sharks fulfill the role of apex predators in the ocean, performing the same function as lions, tigers, and wolves in other ecosystems. As such, they must exert a tremendous influence on populations of animals at lower positions in the food pyramid, and upon the health of the entire system. However, our knowledge of the dynamics of ocean biological systems is at a very primitive state, and does not yet permit us to model interactions between predator and prey populations.

The gill arches of this basking shark (Cetorhinus maximus) *support the gill rakers which strain plankton as the shark swims, mouth wide open.*

It is not surprising, in such a large and diverse group of organisms, that different species have evolved a wide variety of feeding mechanisms and strategies. The two largest species of sharks, whale sharks and basking sharks, are filter-feeders, as are manta and mobula rays (also known as devil rays) and the megamouth shark. Basking sharks are somehow able to locate plankton patches where their preferred

*Leopard shark (*Triakis semifasciata*).*

food (microscopic shellfish known as copepods) is abundant. They feed by swimming along slowly with their mouths wide open, straining the tiny crustaceans out of the water as it sieves out through the gill rakers. They often feed in lines of several sharks, as the turbulence produced by the swimming of each shark seems to improve the feeding efficiency of the animal behind it. A basking shark can filter at least 65,000 ft³ (1850 m³) of water in an hour, removing millions of tiny animals.

Whale sharks, the largest fish in the ocean, also feed on some of the tiniest creatures. Their preferred prey are organisms in the 0.08–0.16 in (2–4 mm) size range. They are able to locate concentrated food

sources by unknown means. Every year whale sharks appear mysteriously off the western coast of Australia to take advantage of the food chain set off by the mass spawning of reef corals. Whale sharks may feed by swimming slowly along and skimming plankton that collects near the surface in windrows due to water circulation patterns. They are also sometimes seen opening and closing their large mouths in a gulping fashion, either while swimming or while hanging head-up in the water, indicating that they may also be able to capture prey by suction feeding.

The suction method is employed by a number of elasmobranchs. By a rapid opening and enlargement of the mouth, water and food items are drawn inside. Angel sharks, wobbegongs, and other bottom-dwellers use a lunge and explosive expansion of the mouth to suck in fish swimming overhead. These 'ambush predators' utilize camouflage to disguise themselves from potential prey. Wobbegongs, with their algae-like skin flaps, may look so much like an encrusted rock that prey will approach looking for a place to hide. Swell sharks also use suction to take in passing fish, but sometimes just lie on the bottom with their mouths open until a fish swims inside. California leopard sharks suck worms out of their burrows like sipping through a straw. More powerful nurse sharks are said to 'vacuum' lobster out of coral heads, and even to be able to suck conch and small giant clams right out of their shells. Ice divers report that Greenland sharks in the Arctic can 'inhale' bait from 3 ft (1 m) away. Large Greenland sharks, which reach at least 21 ft (6.5 m), might be able to suck in a whole ringed seal.

Stingrays sometimes appear to be sucking buried prey out of the sand, but are actually using their bodies as pumps to displace sand so that they can reach the prey with their mouths. Food items include clams and other shells, shrimp-like organisms, brittle stars, and worms. When feeding, they are often accompanied by small jacks or other fishes, which dart forward to seize small organisms flushed out by the ray's excavations. These fish may 'stake out' a ray as their territory and drive away other fish that attempt to forage with the ray. Bat rays use

Spotted wobbegongs (Orectolobus maculatus) are so perfectly camouflaged that prey may swim right up to their mouths unaware, and even attempt to hide underneath the shark, mistaking it for an algae-covered rock. In a flash the mouth gapes open and the unwary organism vanishes inside.

*Whitetip reef sharks (Triaenodon obesus) often ignore healthy fish schooling around them
when searching for the scent of injured fish hiding in coral crevices. The coral provides little protection from
whitetips which can suck their prey out of the reef or break apart the coral to get at their quarry.*

a different technique – blowing jets of water through their mouths to excavate sand and reveal prey. Eagle rays merely plow through the bottom sediments with their upturned snouts.

Manta rays exhibit one of the most unusual feeding methods of any elasmobranch. Flaps called cephalic lobes, which are kept rolled up like pointed horns during travel, are unfurled when feeding to act as scoops directing plankton into the huge terminal mouth. Mantas may skim the surface along windrow lines like whale sharks, but they also frequently feed by executing backwards vertical loops. Somehow the turbulence created by the acrobatics seems to concentrate the plankton so that it can be scooped into the gaping chasm of a mouth and captured on the filter plates.

Thresher sharks also have a remarkable feeding technique. In these distinctive sharks, the upper lobe of the caudal fin is elongated to a length equal to the rest of the body. The sharks use the fin like a whip to herd and stun the small schooling fishes and squid upon which they prey.

Sawfish and saw sharks likewise have specially modified feeding structures. In both of these groups, the rostrum is elongated into a flat sword-like blade with teeth along both edges. The saws are used both to dig in the bottom sand for mollusks and crustaceans, and to slash through schools of fish.

Torpedo rays are very sluggish swimmers, but manage to feed quite effectively with the aid of special organs in their fins which enable them to electrocute their prey. They merely have to glide above an unsuspecting fish. It can then be stunned with a high-voltage jolt from the electric organs and eaten at leisure.

Cookie cutter sharks are suspected of employing a sort of lure. They have luminous organs that cover the undersides of their bodies, except for a dark patch just behind the mouth. Scientists believe that these deep-sea sharks can adjust their light output to match the level of light downwelling from the surface. This renders them almost invisible to animals beneath them which are looking upwards for a dark silhouette. Except, that is, for the dark throat patch which, surrounded by the glow of light-emitting organs, looks like the silhouette of a small fish. This method of attracting in a large predator would explain how they are able to get close enough to their much larger victims to dart forward and sink in their teeth. Once attached, they twist their bodies around to remove a plug of flesh with the ice-cream-scoop-shaped lower jaw. They are known to attack whales, dolphins, squid, elephant seals, large sharks, billfish, and even nuclear submarines. There is at least one case of a cookie cutter feeding on a human, although the person is believed to have drowned prior to the attack.

Some sharks and rays feed in groups. In most cases, these appear to be just a matter of individuals being attracted to the same food source. Cooperative feeding has been recorded in juvenile lemon sharks, which will herd a school of fish into the shoreline, and then take turns feeding on them. Another example could be the 'line swimming' of basking sharks, although this is more likely a case of each shark taking advantage of the one in front of it. Generally, however, group feeding is more competitive than cooperative. In some cases, a hierarchy can be observed, with the more dominant animals feeding first, and subordinates waiting their turn. Smaller animals that attempt to feed out of turn may be threatened or bitten by the larger sharks. In other cases, competition can escalate into a 'feeding frenzy' with sharks snapping wildly at anything in the vicinity in an attempt to get a piece of the food before it is devoured by the others. In such situations, some of the participating sharks may be bitten, and even eaten, by the other sharks.

The majority of sharks are primarily fish-eaters, although they are likely to also take cephalopods (octopus and squid) and crustaceans (crab, lobster, and shrimp) as well. They may follow schools of migrating fish, or patrol areas where currents draw large numbers of prey. Oceanic whitetip sharks are often seen following pods of short-finned pilot whales, although the nature of the association is not well understood. It is possible that the sharks are taking advantage of the pilot whales' remarkable ability to find food (mostly squid) by echolocation.

The sharks may also be feeding on the feces of the whales, or on sick or dying individuals, stillborn calves, afterbirth, etc.

Unlike oceanic whitetip sharks, which cruise the open ocean, whitetip reef sharks are specialists in feeding among the tight spaces of coral reefs. Like many sharks, they concentrate their efforts on fish that are sick or injured. Reef fish, when injured, usually seek shelter within a small chamber under the coral. This gives them protection from most sharks, but not from reef whitetips. With their flattened heads, and slender eel-like bodies, they are able to squeeze into spaces that look much too tight for an animal of that size. If a wounded fish hides in a space too small for them to get into, they will actually break apart the coral to get at the fish.

It has been reported that whitetip reef sharks sometimes cooperate with jack fish to capture smaller schooling fish. The jacks attack the fish school, prompting some of the fish to seek shelter in the reef. The sharks then probe the reef until they either capture the fish, or drive it out where the waiting jacks can catch it.

Mako sharks are reputed to be the fastest fish in the ocean. They are capable of chasing down many types of prey fish by sheer speed and agility.

Great white sharks, by contrast, require the element of surprise to seize prey that may be quicker or more maneuverable than themselves. They often swim along the bottom in order to stalk prey swimming close to the surface, particularly seals and sea lions. It appears that they identify their prey by its dark silhouette against the bright skylight. The shark, however, is camouflaged by its dark back which blends into the dark sea floor, enabling it to move directly under its quarry without detection. It then makes a sudden upward rush, sometimes exiting the water as it seizes its target. White sharks sometimes lift their heads out of the water to look about, and have been reported to snatch resting seals and sea lions off rocks above the water's surface.

Tiger sharks are also known to leave the water in pursuit of their prey, launching themselves onto the beach in pursuit of dolphins and sea turtles, and to feed on stranded whales. Smoothhound sharks sometimes leap onto mud flats to snatch crabs, and blacktip reef sharks are reported to deliberately drive fish onto shore and beach themselves to feed on them.

Most sharks are somewhat flexible in their diets and feeding methods, and will take advantage of various food sources that become available, in order to avoid starvation. For example, blue sharks, which normally feed on mackerel, squid, and other schooling mid-water prey, will also take bottom fish and invertebrates, as well as snatch flying fish, needlefish, and even sea birds at the water's surface. On one occasion when dense swarms of krill formed just under the ocean's surface, blue sharks were seen swimming through the krill with open mouths, gulping down the tiny crustaceans by the thousands.

A few types of sharks, including bull sharks, oceanic whitetip sharks, and most notably tiger sharks, are fairly indiscriminate in their feeding habits. Tiger sharks feed on almost anything that lives in the ocean or falls into it, including jellyfish, crabs, lobster, conch and other shellfish, tunicates (sea squirts), birds, sea snakes, iguanas, turtles, rays, sharks, a great variety of bony fishes, seals, dolphins, horses, cattle, humans, and carrion, including dead hyenas, monkeys, rats, and donkeys. Tiger sharks are sometimes referred to as 'swimming garbage cans'. Because of their lack of discrimination in feeding they are susceptible to ingestion of indigestible junk, and have been found with all kinds of unusual items in their stomachs, reportedly including antlers, coal, wood, a roll of tarpaper, shoes, a keg of nails, a suit of armor, etc. They do not become incapacitated by such refuse because, like all members of their family, they are able to spit their stomachs out and turn them inside out to get rid of indigestible waste. Some of the requiem sharks are also able to evert their intestines through the cloacal opening. In this way they can both eject debris from the lower part of the digestive tract, and also possibly wash off tapeworms and other parasites.

Although the image of tiger sharks as lazy carrion feeders is

Blue sharks (Prionace glauca) are highly adaptable open ocean predators which feed on everything from tiny krill to whale carcasses. These blue sharks herded a school of anchovy into a tight ball, then swam through it with open mouths, sometimes seizing several fish at once.

sometimes true, they can also be skillful predators. By unknown methods, tiger sharks time their annual arrival in the lagoons of the NW Hawaiian Islands to coincide precisely with the fledging of baby albatrosses. When young birds fail to get airborne on their first attempt, they often fall into the lagoon – and the waiting jaws of a tiger shark. The sharks appear to be able to track the birds through the air so that they can position themselves directly beneath when a bird lands in the water.

Many sharks and rays change their feeding habits as they mature. As skates in the North Sea grow, for example, they switch from feeding mainly on crustaceans to a fish-based diet. Changes in diet may be reflected in changes in the shape of the teeth as the animal grows. Young mako sharks have slender teeth, designed for seizing small fish, to be swallowed whole. As they age, the upper teeth broaden, and become more flattened and triangular – better adapted for slicing apart larger food items, such as swordfish and large sharks.

The design of the teeth varies greatly among the different sharks and rays and is highly indicative of the diet and feeding habits of the species. Sand tigers have curved needle-like teeth ideally designed for seizing and holding soft-bodied fish. Great whites have large serrated triangular teeth which can saw through the flesh, tendons, and bones of their mammalian prey. The cobblestone-like jaws of horn sharks are ideal for crushing sea urchins, barnacles, sea stars, and crabs. The serrated, cockscomb-shaped teeth of tiger sharks can slice right through the shell of a sea turtle, one of their favorite delicacies. Cownose rays have flat tooth plates for smashing hard-shelled mollusks and crustaceans. The toothplates of eagle rays are said to be strong enough to break open a conch. After crushing a sea shell, the eagle ray spits out the whole mass, and then reingests only the soft parts. Manta rays, basking sharks, and whale sharks have tiny vestigial teeth which are not used for feeding at all, as that function has been taken over by the gill rakers in basking sharks, filter

plates in mantas, and a sponge-like mesh of connective tissue in whale sharks.

Some fossil teeth from very ancient sharks are worn and blunt, probably affecting the feeding efficiency of those sharks as they aged. But teeth of modern sharks and recent fossils are almost always in perfect condition, regardless of the age of the shark. It's not unusual for a fossil hunter to slice open a finger on a shark's tooth that is millions of years old. This is because teeth are shed and replaced on a regular basis, before they can be worn down by use. Behind the erect, functional row of teeth are multiple back-ups, constantly moving forward as if on a conveyor belt. The replacement rows are staggered, so not all of the teeth are replaced at once, except in a few deep-sea sharks (such as the cookie cutter) which have the lower teeth interlocked to function as a unit. And there is no evidence that a replacement tooth can pop right up if a functional tooth is lost. The teeth seem to move forward at a fixed rate. This rate, however, varies with the age of the shark. Young sharks replace teeth rapidly as they grow and their diet changes. They may get a new set of teeth every week or two. White shark embryos may go through four or more sets of teeth while still in the womb. Older sharks replace teeth less often, perhaps once or twice a year. It still amounts to a staggering amount of teeth over a shark's lifetime. It is estimated that a requiem shark can produce 20,000 teeth over a 25-year period (and some live much longer than 25 years)! It is no wonder that shark teeth are the most common fossils on earth.

Most elasmobranchs will respond to a food stimulus at any time of day if they are hungry. But many have preferred hunting times. Tiger sharks, whitetip reef sharks, and nurse sharks, for example, are most active at night. Whitetip reef sharks and nurse sharks can often be seen resting on the bottom, in caves or ledges, during the day. Other sharks, such as lemon sharks, are most active around dawn and dusk.

The broad, serrated teeth of tiger sharks (Galeocerdo cuvier) *enable them to easily rip apart large prey and carrion, such as this marlin carcass.*

Strategies for Survival

Surviving in a rough-and-tumble environment like the ocean requires more than just getting enough to eat. Elasmobranchs must also, like any other organisms, escape the many enemies that might take advantage of them. The struggle for survival starts even before birth. Eggs and embryos of mackerel sharks and their relatives are at risk from their own siblings. The first sharks to hatch consume all of the remaining eggs in the uterus. Some types of sharks and rays attach their eggs to the ocean floor and leave them to develop outside the body, sometimes for as long as a year. During this time, the egg has no protection other than the horny case which encapsulates it. The large eggs may be eaten by fish, but the worst threat is from marine snails, which drill through the egg case and suck out the yolk.

As soon as it emerges from the egg case or the birth canal (depending on the mode of reproduction of the particular species), the shark (or ray) is in even more danger. Small elasmobranchs are a favored food of many types of large sharks and may even be preyed upon by members of their own species, as well as by bony fish, wading birds, crocodiles, etc. Most immediately seek some sort of sheltered habitat. Baby lemon sharks, for example, dash into the mangrove swamps at the edge of the lagoons where they are born, and hide among the roots.

Hiding and camouflage are primary defense strategies for many elasmobranchs throughout their lives. Many rays and bottom-dwelling sharks lie flat on the bottom, or bury themselves partially or completely in the bottom sediments. Bottom-dwellers that don't have flat bodies, such as Port Jackson and other horn sharks, have color patterns that enable them to blend in with the bottom rocks. Wobbegongs have fleshy tassels that look like seaweed, and render them almost invisible against the right background. Some sharks use disruptive coloration, such as spots and stripes, which break up the shape of the animal and make it less conspicuous. Such patterns help to camouflage everything from baby nurse sharks a half-meter long to full-grown whale sharks 50 ft (15 m) long. Even sharks that swim in the open ocean use camouflage, in the form of counter-shading. A dark upper body enables the shark to blend with the dark depths when viewed from above, while a light underside matches the sky light when viewed from below.

Some sharks can actually change their color. Blacktip sharks, ordinarily gray, blanch to nearly pure white when hiding within patches of milky white water on shallow banks in the Bahamas. When removed from those patches of water, they quickly regain their normal gray color. Even more remarkable are some small deep-water dogfish sharks whose bodies are covered with small light organs. These organs can apparently emit a glow that matches the background light from the sun, and prevent the shark from creating a silhouette that could be targeted by a larger predator attacking from underneath.

Teeth can be a defensive, as well as offensive, tool. Many normally docile sharks will not hesitate to bite if threatened. In Florida, a preponderance of shark bites on skin divers are inflicted by the 'harmless' nurse shark, because of the difficulty some foolish divers have in resisting the urge to yank on the tail of a shark found resting on the bottom.

While nurse sharks tend to clamp down on an attacker (and sometimes have to be removed from the water before they can be pried loose), many sharks defend themselves with a slashing bite or a quick bite and release. Examination of bite wounds on humans leads some experts to suggest that most shark 'attacks' may actually be shark 'defenses'. Some species of sharks signal their intent to defend

This juvenile horn shark (Heterodontus francisci) is a sluggish swimmer, but has sharp spines in front of each dorsal fin to discourage predation.

themselves, their 'individual space', or their food with an aggressive display. This display is most dramatic in the gray reef shark, which lifts its snout and arches its back in an S-curve, while twisting from side to side, with its pectoral fins pointed down.

Some species also use fin spines for defense. Juvenile horn sharks share habitat with angel sharks in California, and are prone to being gulped up by a hidden angel shark. The erect dorsal spines jab the predator in the roof of the mouth, and it spits out the horn shark, often unharmed.

The dorsal spines of stingrays, eagle rays, and bat rays have been modified into tail barbs, with associated venom glands. When attacked or threatened a stingray is likely to arch its back and thrust a barb into the aggressor. This somehow does not seem to discourage hammerhead sharks, which have been found with dozens of stingray barbs embedded in their mouths and throats. The dual defenses of stingrays, camouflage and tail barbs, present a particular hazard to humans. Stingrays buried under the sand in shallow water may not be seen by waders. When stepped upon, the stingray reacts by driving a barb into the foot or leg which has molested it. The venom introduced with the barb is likely to cause necrosis, resulting in a wound that may take months to heal. Fishers are exposed to greater danger because when handling nets they may be struck in the upper body by a stingray barb, and receive an injury, or a secondary infection, which can be fatal. Stingrays are responsible for a much higher number of injuries to humans than are sharks. Statistics on fatalities are not kept, but these are believed to be rare.

Whiprays have long tails which are covered with sharp thorns. The tail can be lashed like a whip to lacerate an attacker.

The defensive method of torpedo rays appears to be even more effective. A powerful electric jolt, from electric organs within the pectoral 'wings', seems to discourage most attacks. The voltage of these discharges has been measured at up to 50 volts in the water, and over 200 volts out of the water. The in-air measurements may not be meaningful, as electric current is dissipated quickly in sea water, but there are anecdotal reports of divers being knocked unconscious by a torpedo ray discharge. The consequences could be even worse, as the frequency and voltage of the discharge are similar to that used for human heart defibrillation. There are few records of predation upon this group. The fact that they still use camouflage, and are occasionally found in the stomach of a large shark, though, indicates that even this defense is not 100 per cent effective.

Some sharks are deadly when eaten, although it is unlikely that this is due to an evolved anti-predation factor. Some cases of shark poisoning have been blamed upon ciguatera toxin. This is a 'food chain poison' which is produced by a microorganism that grows on marine algae. The algae are consumed by fish, which are eaten by larger fish, and so forth, with the poison being concentrated more at each step in the food chain. In some cases, ciguatera has been ruled out, and the poisoning has been blamed on compounds called 'carchatoxins' (or 'shark poisons'). Like ciguatera, this poison likely travels up the food chain to sharks. Shark poisoning is often fatal. In one outbreak, 98 people died. However, it is rare enough that few predators, apart from humans in some cases, are likely to learn to avoid eating sharks for this reason.

The flesh of one shark, the Greenland shark, is almost always toxic. The poison has not been positively identified, but it has been suggested that the cause is a digestive product of one of the ammonia-like chemicals that sharks use to regulate their osmotic balance (see *Living in the Sea* chapter).

Size is one of the best defenses. Sharks that are born at a relatively large size, such as the sand tiger, which is already 3 ft (1 m) long when it leaves the womb, have a tremendous advantage against predation. The larger an animal grows, the safer it is. However, even very large sharks cannot swim the ocean in total security. A 9 ft (2.75 m) lemon shark was once found in the stomach of a 15 ft (4.5 m) great hammerhead. Hammerheads, in turn, are sometimes eaten by orcas (killer whales). Orcas have also been seen feeding on Galapagos sharks, mako sharks, and even a great white shark. Only the liver of the white shark was consumed.

*The reticulate whipray (Himantura uarnak) has not only a sting to defend itself,
but also a long thin tail covered with a large number of small sharp thorns. The tail
can be flailed like a whip in self-defense. Its main enemies are larger sharks.*

Some sharks and rays aggregate together, even when not feeding. A few swim in true schools. (In a school the individuals face the same direction, are evenly spaced, and swim at the same speed.) Schooling species include scalloped hammerhead sharks, cownose rays, eagle rays, and mobula rays. Schools and aggregations may serve social functions, such as facilitating mating, but they likely diminish the threat of predation as well. Schools of scalloped hammerheads disperse at night for feeding, but reform by day when the sharks are resting. The two greatest potential threats to these animals (apart from humans) are orcas and white sharks, which are both visual predators, so schooling by day makes sense as a defensive strategy.

Not all of the enemies of elasmobranchs are larger animals. The diminutive 1 ft 7 in (0.5 m) cookie cutter shark attacks large sharks, including megamouth sharks, as well as marine mammals and bony fishes.

The worst enemies can be even smaller. Like all animals, elasmobranchs are subject to the ravages of parasites and disease organisms. Sharks and rays suffer infestations of many different internal and external parasites, including barnacles, copepods and isopods (small crustaceans), leeches, flatworms, tapeworms, and 'vampire snails' – mollusks which attack certain species, such as torpedo rays and nurse sharks, while they are resting. The 'vampires' do not live permanently on their host, but attack it opportunistically, reaching over with a long siphon tube to pierce it and suck out body juices. Parasites are so ubiquitous that scientists have even been able to use them as biological 'markers' to study life history parameters, migration ranges, and genetic characters of the host animals.

Some sharks carry heavy loads of parasites, and are still able to function, but the infestations undoubtedly affect the health and lifespan of the animal. Individuals which are able to rid themselves of parasites stand a better chance of survival than those that do not. Accordingly, elasmobranchs have formed interesting partnerships with other animals which can assist them in the parasite control department. Many sharks and rays are accompanied by sharksuckers, or remoras, which attach themselves to their host by a flattened sucking disc on top of the head. The relationship between the host elasmobranch and its suckerfish cohorts is a complex one that includes consumption of ectoparasites by the suckerfish.

Even rays and sharks which are carrying several remoras also visit cleaning stations in order to access the services of other cleaning fishes. The cleaning stations can be at fixed locations on the reef, or may be found under floating kelp paddies or other drifting shelters. Sharks that may normally feed on fish the same size as the cleaners suspend their predatory instincts at these stations, and allow a variety of smaller fishes to range over their bodies, and even pick parasites from around their mouths. The cleaning fish get an easy meal in return for servicing the larger one. Manta rays usually approach cleaning stations in an upcurrent direction, so that they can 'stall out' with the current holding their bodies up while they are cleaned. Sharks that are not able to ventilate their gills while resting on the bottom glide slowly through a cleaning station while they are serviced, coming nearly to a stop, but flipping the tail again before they start to sink. The cleaner fish will often rush out several meters or more from the safety of the reef to greet a shark or manta and begin cleaning it. The shark or ray will often signal its readiness to be cleaned with a special body posture.

Pelagic sharks, such as blues and makos, typically have more visible external parasites than do reef sharks. This may be because of reduced access to cleaning stations. They may depend upon cleaners living in kelp paddies, which are short-lived refuges that may also move long distances from day to day. Even pelagic species such as the pelagic thresher shark will visit cleaning stations on reefs associated with offshore islands within their range. Sedentary elasmobranchs undoubtedly receive the best cleaning services, though. Cleaning organisms,

These golden cownose rays (Rhinoptera steindachneri) *in the Galapagos find protection in numbers by schooling. Few elasmobranchs form true schools.*

including cleaner shrimp, as well as fish, may stay on them for hours, or return to them repeatedly while they rest on the bottom.

The cleaning relationship may provide a major part of the solution to the 'mystery of the sleeping sharks'. When Caribbean reef sharks (*Carcharhinus perezi*) were found resting on the bottom in caves in Mexico, scientists were mystified, because other species of sleek-bodied requiem sharks swim continuously. It was speculated that there was some special characteristic of the water in the caves that was attractive to the sharks, but tests revealed no differences from the sea water outside the caves. Subsequently, it was discovered that resting on the bottom is a characteristic of this species throughout its range. Closer observation revealed that the sharks were sometimes attended by cleaner fish while resting.

Severe infestations of parasites, or invasion of the body by pathogenic microbes such as bacteria, viruses, and fungi, can produce disease symptoms. The ocean is an unforgiving environment, and a disease does not have to kill its victim directly in order to be fatal. Any weakness or change in behavior is likely to be immediately noticed by other members of the community. Although many diseases of elasmobranchs are recorded in captivity, it is rare to see an obviously sick individual in the ocean. This is because any that exhibit obvious signs of weakness disappear rather quickly – usually down the throat of a larger shark.

In such a thrive-or-die regimen, possession of a powerful immune system is essential to survival. Elasmobranchs were once thought to lack T cells, but recent research shows that they do have T cells, and that these function in essentially the same way as those of humans. Sharks and rays also have B cells – the other essential component of our two-part immune system, but these operate in a somewhat different way than ours to provide immunity to a wide range of diseases.

One of the most intriguing aspects of the elasmobranch immune system is their apparent high resistance to tumor formation. Tumors are clusters of abnormal cells that grow at an exceptionally high rate. To feed this rapid growth, they require a dense development of blood vessels. Blood vessels do not form within cartilage, leading some to speculate that the cartilaginous skeletons of elasmobranchs are somehow responsible for inhibiting tumor growth. Researchers have been testing various extracts of shark cartilage to see if a compound can be isolated which might have the property of preventing growth of blood vessels, and thus be of potential use for suppressing tumors in other animals. Some of the compounds isolated do seem to have the property of inhibiting growth of blood vessels. However the researchers believe that the resistance of elasmobranchs to tumor formation is most likely due to their immune systems, and not related to the cartilage in their skeletons. Squalamine, a compound which was originally discovered in sharks, but is now synthesized, also appears to inhibit the growth of blood vessels that feed developing tumors, and may have antibiotic properties as well. Clinical tests are underway.

Without waiting for results from the ongoing research, commercial interests have jumped in and begun marketing shark cartilage capsules as a cancer cure. Recent tests on humans have shown that taking these pills has no effect on the development of cancer other than to divert financial resources that might otherwise be used for more effective treatments. Researchers say that any specific compounds which inhibit the growth of blood vessels in shark cartilage would probably not be able to pass through the human digestive system, and do not appear to be absorbed when eaten. Nonetheless, hundreds of thousands of sharks are now being ground up annually to produce cartilage pills. It is ironic that the potent immune system that has protected elasmobranchs from countless threats and enabled them to continue to evolve for hundreds of millions of years could now be a cause of their undoing.

The remora on this whale shark (Rhincodon typus) *obtains free transportation. The shark benefits by having its parasites consumed.*

Genetic Transport into the Future

Survival accomplishes nothing, evolutionarily, if an animal doesn't leave offspring. All creatures eventually die, but a good set of genes can live forever. To attain immortality and project themselves into the future, animals must reproduce. One of the defining characters of the Chondrichthyes is their method of reproduction. It is the key to both their past evolutionary success and their current state of crisis.

All chondrichthyans practice internal fertilization. In other words, they mate. Most bony fishes spawn. When fish spawn they release large numbers of eggs and sperm into the water. Some sperm manage to find and fertilize an egg. In some cases, the eggs are tended, but most species just allow their eggs to drift off in the current, joining the buffet for all the hungry little creatures in the plankton. Only a few will survive to become adults and produce offspring themselves.

The key to success for fish that spawn is producing lots of eggs – sometimes millions to hundreds of millions of eggs per year. The cartilaginous fishes have adopted an entirely different strategy – one that has been extremely successful for mammals and reptiles as well. Instead of producing many small eggs, a shark or ray produces a few large ones. These eggs are not cast out into the environment, but retained within the female's body. The male must inject sperm into her body to fertilize the eggs. All, or part, of the period of development of the embryo can then take place within the female's body, where it is safe from most predation and other threats. The embryo is either carried to term within the female, or deposited within a protective egg case in a suitable location on the bottom. In either case, when the pup emerges, it is already in an appropriate habitat. And it has already attained a size that will protect it from the vast majority of the hungry mouths in the ocean. It is estimated that about half of young lemon sharks survive their first year of life. This is a very high survival rate compared to mass spawners, for

which the figure may be a fraction of one per cent.

The trade-off for providing the offspring with such tremendously improved chances of survival is that only a few offspring can be produced. So much energy must be invested in each one that it is impossible to produce large numbers, as spawners do. Also, to produce large eggs and/or give birth to a large pup, the mother must reach a large size herself before reproducing. Most elasmobranchs require a much longer time to reach maturity than do most bony fishes. Animals that have made the reproductive 'choice' of quality over quantity of offspring are referred to by ecologists as 'k-selected' species.

This reproductive strategy has great advantages, as long as the status quo is maintained in the ocean, and mortality is low. But when something changes, and a die-off occurs, k-selected species are at a disadvantage. Their slow growth, delayed maturity, and low reproductive rates do not allow them to recover rapidly. It may take many decades for a population to return to former levels. On the other hand, mass spawners can recover from a major mortality event in a single season, if environmental conditions are right. Only a few surviving adults can produce millions of fertile eggs. In these species, it is not the number of reproducing adults, but the conditions affecting survival of the eggs and larvae, that determine the future of the population.

Because of their rapid recovery potential, mass spawners do well in unstable or changing environments. K-selected animals, such as sharks, thrive in stable environments. For most of their evolutionary history, until quite recently, their environment has been relatively stable, and this mode of reproduction has served them well.

To accomplish internal fertilization, male sharks and rays have claspers which are analogous to the penis in a mammal. One obvious difference is that elasmobranchs have two. Normally, only one is inserted

A baby swell shark (Cephaloscyllium ventriosum) *emerges from its egg case 7 to 10 months after the case was deposited on the sea floor.*

into the female during mating. Some claspers have spines or hooks to anchor them in the female's body. The two claspers are on the underside of the body, between the two pelvic fins, and point to the rear when not in use. The female's genital opening is in approximately the same location, and joins the anus in a slit called the cloaca.

For a male to insert a clasper into the female's cloaca requires a flexing and rotation of the clasper, plus some contortions. He must either twist the rear part of his body around to reach under her, or he must flip her over, or get his whole body beneath hers, upside-down. All of these techniques are used by elasmobranchs. And all require the male to maintain contact with the female. Lacking any hands to hold her with, he usually accomplishes this with his teeth.

The use of teeth to seize and hold a female during copulation presents a risk of injury, especially in those species with large sharp teeth. In some species, the males also slash and nip at the females prior to mating. The biting may be a necessary part of 'foreplay', which prompts the female's cooperation and in some species may even trigger ovulation. The female sometimes suffers deep and extensive punctures and lacerations. There are some accounts of female rays suffering fatal injuries during mating. However, most heal quickly. The risk is reduced by adaptations such as thicker skin on females. In blue sharks, the skin on the backs of females is twice as thick as on males.

In most rays, and some sharks, the teeth of males and females are shaped differently, with the females having more rounded teeth, and the males having pointed teeth. The diet is not known to vary between the sexes, so the most likely explanation is that the males require sharper teeth to hold onto the females during mating. Male Atlantic stingrays actually change their tooth shape during the year, developing a pointed cusp in the mating season, while retaining a molar-like shape during the rest of the year. Another difference between the sexes is that, in most species of elasmobranchs, females grow larger than males.

Apart from the danger of injuring each other, mating elasmobranchs suffer hazards associated with having to assume an undignified position while swimming. Scalloped hammerheads, among the most

negatively buoyant of sharks, have been seen to drop 20 ft (6 m) and crash into the reef while mating. Whitetip reef sharks have been photographed mating with their heads pressed down against the coral. Epaulette sharks have been observed rolling over a bed of sharp staghorn coral while mating. There is also an increased risk of predation while preoccupied with mating. And males may be injured by females which resist their advances. Female round stingrays use their tail barbs to lance males that bite them in an attempt to copulate, and female sand tiger sharks sometimes turn and bite the male back during courtship attempts. Additionally, males may be injured by other males competing for access to the same female.

Considering the perils of copulation and the investment in time and energy required to carry an embryo through gestation, and given that very few offspring are produced, it would be expected that females might be very particular about which males they accept as mates. It would not be surprising to find a courtship procedure that would select the fittest and strongest males. The few observations which have been made of courtship and mating in elasmobranchs do seem to validate this prediction.

One of the best-studied elasmobranch mating systems is that of the nurse shark, *Ginglymostoma cirratum*. These normally languid sharks congregate in shallow lagoons during the breeding season. Females resist the mating attempts of all but the largest, strongest males, and may retreat to very shallow water to discourage unwanted suitors. A male will attempt to capture a female by seizing her pectoral fin in his mouth and dragging her to deeper water where he can flip her over for mating. To be successful, he must be fit indeed, as he is unable to pump water over his gills, and is thus deprived of oxygen, for the entire time that he has her fin in his mouth. Additionally the female resists by digging her other pectoral fin into the bottom. Less than 10 per cent of mating attempts are successful. Smaller males may boost their success by working in teams of two to six to subdue a female and get her into deep enough water. Generally the biggest, most aggressive, and most dominant males are the most successful.

Female scalloped hammerheads (Sphyrna lewini) form schools by day throughout the year.
At night the schools break up as the sharks disperse to feed. One function of the schools appears to be to
facilitate courtship and mating. Schooling may also reduce the risk of predation by larger sharks and orcas.

Male nurse sharks (Ginglymostoma cirratum) follow a female during courtship. In order to produce offspring with the best available genes, females require males to compete and prove their fitness before mating. By resisting, the female ensures that only the strongest males will father her pups.

Various cues are used to indicate intent and receptivity to other members of the species. It is believed that in most elasmobranchs the females release pheromones, or scent signals, which the males can detect. Male sharks and rays are sometimes seen following females, with their snouts close to the cloaca. Male southern stingrays react instantly to the release of an extract of stingray ovaries, and swim in the direction of the source. In mating aggregations of round stingrays, females which are not receptive bury themselves, while those which are receptive lie on the surface in groups. Manta rays form 'chains' consisting of a female pursued by a line of males, with the whole group performing complicated acrobatic maneuvers. It is likely that a selection process is occurring that somehow enables the female to end up with the fittest mate.

Many species segregate by sex and size except when mingling for reproductive purposes. Scalloped hammerheads form schools that consist mostly of females. The females compete for positions, close to the center of the school. The larger, more dominant females attain these favored positions, and enforce them by slamming with open jaws into subordinates that move in too close. The center positions may be safer from predators, but the primary advantage seems to be access to males. When males enter the school, they go to the center to mate.

In most sharks and rays, fertilization occurs immediately after mating. However, in some species, including tope, blue, and dusky sharks, the sperm can be stored and used for months to years after mating.

If mating is successful, and eggs are fertilized, they develop according to one of at least eight different patterns, depending upon the species. Some types of elasmobranchs encase each fertilized egg in a protective pouch and deposit the cases on the ocean floor. The developing embryo takes its nourishment from a large yolk, which is consumed as the embryo grows. When fully developed, the embryo forces its way out by splitting open the egg case. Approximately 43 per cent of the known species of cartilaginous fish are egg-layers. This includes all skates and chimaeras, horn sharks, swell sharks, cat sharks, and some others.

Egg cases are distinctive for each species. Some have tendrils which the mother uses to attach the case to some feature on the bottom. Others have sticky fibers along the sides, providing a Velcro-like attachment. The egg cases of horn sharks are auger-shaped. Apparently the mother uses her mouth or tail to wedge them into the bottom while they are still soft. Then the flanges harden and hold the case in place. The egg cases of skates are shaped like handbags, and are known as 'mermaids' purses' when they wash up on the beach.

In the other 57 per cent of elasmobranch species, the embryos develop within the mother, and are born live, fully developed, and ready to live on their own. Some species, notably nurse sharks and whale sharks, enclose the eggs in heavy egg cases, like those of egg-laying sharks. The egg cases are not deposited though, and the pup hatches from the case within the mother, prior to being born. The embryo is believed to receive all of its nutrition from the egg yolk, and none directly from the mother. This is also thought to be true of some other species, such as tiger sharks, which do not sheath the egg in a case.

In a few sharks and most or all rays, the mother secretes a nutritious fluid called 'uterine milk', which is consumed by the embryos. In stingrays, eagle rays, and butterfly rays, extensions of the uterus reach through the spiracle to deliver uterine milk directly to the gut of the embryo. In others, the uterine secretions are absorbed through the skin. A newborn can weigh up to 50 times as much as the unfertilized egg, indicating that most of the nourishment is coming from the uterine secretions, rather than the egg yolk.

In members of the mackerel shark group, including great white, mako, porbeagle, sand tiger, and thresher sharks, embryos supplement their own yolk supply by consuming other eggs within the womb. Females of some species produce thousands of 'nutritive eggs' as a food supply for the few embryos which actually develop. In sand tigers, the largest embryo in each uterus consumes its smaller siblings, as well as unfertilized eggs. Therefore only two pups are born at a time – one from each uterus. While the teeth of many sharks do not erupt until after birth, the teeth of sand tiger embryos erupt when they are only 2½ in (6 cm) long. White shark embryos also have erupted teeth, but apparently feed only on undeveloped eggs, and not on other embryos. White sharks have been captured with up to 14 embryos inside.

In requiem sharks and hammerheads the developing embryo is nourished directly from the mother's bloodstream via a structure very similar to the mammalian placenta. These more recently evolved families comprise about 9 per cent of elasmobranch species. Some nourish the embryo with uterine milk as well as through the placenta. The embryo gets nearly all of its nourishment directly from the mother, rather than from yolk. The most extreme example is the small spadenose shark, which has essentially no yolk in the tiny eggs of only 0.04 in (1 mm) diameter. By contrast, the eggs of some egg-laying and egg-retaining species rank among the largest cells known in the animal kingdom.

Placental sharks expel an afterbirth, consisting of the placenta and embryonic membranes, along with the pup. In lemon sharks it has been observed that sharksuckers (remoras) gather on pregnant females and feed on the afterbirth during pupping. Some pups are born with the umbilical cord still attached, and the sharksuckers may actually assist the birth by breaking and eating the cord.

Many types of elasmobranchs seek out special nursery areas to give birth. These are often in lagoons, bays, and estuaries – places where the young will be able to find plenty of food, and will also be able to find places to hide from larger sharks which might eat them. A few species, however, move farther offshore to give birth. Pregnant females often cease feeding when they enter the nurseries, reducing the likelihood that they will eat their own young. There are anecdotal accounts of females chasing male sharks away from nurseries. Some egg-laying sharks, such as the Port Jackson, and other horn sharks, use communal nesting sites, returning each year to deposit their egg cases next to those of other members of their species.

In most species, the female's investment in the survival of her offspring ends at the time the pup is born, or the egg case deposited. However, there is one study showing that fresh water stingray females found in the Amazon basin carry their young for 3 to 4 days after birth. There may be other instances, yet to be discovered, of parental care in elasmobranchs, but it is certainly rare and limited.

After deposition, the eggs of egg-laying species take 3 to 15 months to develop and hatch. Live-bearing species have a wide range of gestation periods. In rays, gestation lasts only 2 to 4 months. In sharks it ranges from 5 to 6 months for the spadenose shark and bonnethead, up to two years for the spiny dogfish. The gestation periods for frilled sharks and basking sharks are undetermined, but may be as long as three-and-a-half years; 10 to 12 months is typical for most sharks.

Some elasmobranchs reproduce on an annual cycle, but many produce young only every two or three years. The number of young produced is usually quite small, but varies considerably from species to species. Horn sharks deposit only two egg capsules at a time – one per ovary – but repeat at two-week intervals during the four-month breeding season. Sand tigers also produce one pup per ovary, but breed only once every other year, and so average one pup per year. The gulper shark bears only a single pup at a time. At the other end of the spectrum, blue sharks can have litters of up to 132 pups, and one whale shark was taken with 307 embryos inside. The dozen or so pups that a lemon shark bears every other year is fairly typical for live-bearing sharks.

Elasmobranchs tend to be long-lived, slow-growing animals that take a long time to reach maturity. Bull sharks, for instance, do not give birth until they reach an age of 18 years, and for bronze whalers, it is 19 to 20 years. Females in some populations of spiny dogfish take 35 years to reach sexual maturity. Even small, fast-growing sharks take 2 to 10 years to reach maturity. In some species the number of offspring increases with the size of the mother, so it may take even longer before an individual reaches its full reproductive potential. The combination of slow growth, delayed maturity, and low fecundity (rate of reproduction) means that most sharks and rays can produce only a small number of offspring during a fairly long life. Therefore if a population is impacted by fishing, or some other cause of high mortality, it may take many, many years to recover, or not recover at all.

A young lemon shark (Negaprion brevirostris), *approximately one year of age, cruises through a sea grass bed in a shallow tropical lagoon bordered by mangrove trees. Pregnant lemon sharks come to such locations to give birth. The pups are born live, and immediately flee to the edge of the lagoon, where they hide among the mangrove roots. As they grow, they slowly expand their home range onto the grass flats, and eventually out to the coral reef and into deep water as adults.*

*Of the more than 1000 species of sharks and rays, the great white shark
(Carcharodon carcharias) is among the very few which pose any threat to humans. It is
also among the many species which are threatened by humans. Each year, for every human killed
by a shark, 20 million sharks are killed by humans. White sharks have received legal protection in
Australia, the Maldives, Namibia, South Africa, and the U.S.A. due to declining populations caused
by trophy hunting, commercial and sport fishing, and entrapment in beach mesh nets.*

Human Attack!

In his 1952 book, *Harpoon Venture*, respected British author Gavin Maxwell describes his first sighting of a basking shark — one of the most remarkable, mysterious, and awe-inspiring creatures ever to dwell upon our planet. His first view is of the forward dorsal fin jutting a meter out of the water like a 'great black sail'. Then he spots the second dorsal 20 ft (6 m) behind, moving in a seemingly independent fashion. 'It was some seconds before my brain would acknowledge that these two fins must belong to the same creature', he writes. 'The impact of this realization was tremendous and indescribable: a muddle of excitement in which fear and a sort of exultation were uppermost, as though this were a moment for which I had been unconsciously waiting a long time'. Pulling his boat up to the shark, he is able to see it clearly through the slick calm water of a still afternoon. He describes his astonishment as being as though he had seen a dinosaur. Then he does a typically human thing: he loads two magazines into a machine gun and fires 300 rounds into the shark.

Maxwell was not the only well-known author of his time to machine-gun sharks. The walls of Ernest Hemingway's favorite watering hole in the Bahamas are plastered with photos of him using a tommy gun to dispatch sharks attracted by his fishing activities (which often involved catching and discarding large numbers of marlin and other game fish). Such 'fun' was considered both manly and sporting at the time. Shark-fishing tournaments often resulted in the slaughter of hundreds of animals which were photographed and then either dumped back into the sea or hauled off to the rubbish heap. Environmental ethics have made such rapid inroads over the last decade or two that it is easy to forget that, for most of man's history, the prevailing ethic has been, 'if it moves — kill it'. Indeed, this is still a prevalent attitude in some parts of human society.

Sharks and rays do worse than move, though. A few of the more than 1000 species have the defensive and/or offensive equipment to inflict serious injury or death upon humans that either molest them or just happen to be in the wrong place at the wrong time. These are of course very rare events. Shark bites are much less common than bites from dogs, cats, pigs, squirrels, hamsters, rabbits, raccoons, rats, and other humans. More people are eaten by lions and tigers. More deaths are caused by deer and by honey bees. The chance of being killed by lightning in the coastal states of the U.S.A. is more than 100 times greater than the chance of being killed by a shark. Regardless of statistics, the occasional damage inflicted upon one of our kind has been sufficient motivation for the killing of untold millions of mostly harmless elasmobranchs. Apart from gratuitous 'revenge' killings, several thousand sharks are killed each year as a result of bather protection measures. Beaches in parts of Australia and South Africa are 'protected' for swimmers by use of 'shark mesh' nets or baited hooks. The nets do not form a barrier or screen sharks away from the beaches; they merely reduce numbers of sharks in the area by killing them, along with sea turtles, dolphins, dugongs, and other creatures.

To add to their plight, many species of sharks and rays are good to eat or have other products which are useful to humans. The skin can be turned into high-quality leather, or a substitute for sandpaper. The liver contains large amounts of oil, from which vitamin A can be extracted. The oil is also used in medicines, cosmetics, as a lubricant, for fuel, and for a variety of other purposes. The teeth, jaws, and spines are utilized for weapons, jewelry, and ornaments. The fins are converted into soup. Or the whole body may merely be chopped up and used as bait to catch crabs or some other type of seafood. A number of shark products are being tested for various medicinal purposes, including corneas for human eye transplants, and squalamine and cartilage extracts for anti-tumor therapy and other treatments. In many parts of the world, sharks are now the most valuable fishery product under exploitation. The thousands killed each year as a result of fear and malice are almost insignificant compared to the much larger number that die due to the more powerful motivations of hunger and greed.

Given the combination of killing for sport, fear, revenge, food, and for various industrial and medical products, it may seem surprising that large numbers of elasmobranchs were able to survive into the late twentieth century. The explanation has nothing to do with human restraint, but merely reflects the instability of commercial markets, and the lack of adequate technology to fully exploit the resource. Sharks in the Florida Keys got a reprieve when a blight killed off the sponges, destroying the market for shark liver oil, which the spongers used to throw on the water to enable them to see the bottom more clearly. A number of populations were spared when vitamin A was synthesized. Some fisheries were pursued to the point of collapse, but the majority of species were distributed too far out to sea or too deep, or were just too much trouble to catch to make them worth going after.

In the 1970s things began to change rapidly for elasmobranchs. Motion pictures featuring oversized mechanical sharks created a worldwide hysteria, which reinforced the extant culture of fear and loathing of sharks, leading to a surge of 'human attacks'. Shark meat, which had previously been considered inferior food in many developed countries, suddenly became a trendy menu item. Most importantly, the Chinese economy began a rapid expansion.

Shark-fin soup is a traditional Chinese dish dating back thousands of years. To the western mind, the concept is as inexplicable as bird's nest soup or thousand-year-old eggs. To create the product, shark fins are first dried, then the supporting collagen fibers are extracted from them. After some preparation, these are added to the soup, and take on a consistency similar to noodles. The fibers contribute some texture to the final product, but almost nothing in the way of flavor or nutritional value. The flavor is provided by the soup stock, which is usually built on a chicken and vegetable base. The main difference between shark-fin soup and chicken noodle soup is the price. As more

people in Taiwan, Hong Kong, and mainland China moved out of poverty, there was a large increase in the amount of disposable cash available for such 'luxury' food items. Additionally, larger numbers of westerners who wanted to appear adventurous, began to order the soup. As many traditional fisheries around the world began to collapse from overfishing, government fisheries' offices encouraged fishers to enter the shark-fin trade, and often offered loans, subsidies, or other financial or logistical support for them to convert to this lucrative new fishery. This was done without consideration for the long-term prospects for a fishery based on a resource with a low intrinsic rate of growth.

At about the same time, some unscrupulous promoters learned of the research indicating that substances within cartilage can block the development of blood vessels, which are necessary to support the growth of tumors. Some hastily written promotional books and a media blitz of press releases and television appearances created an instant market for shark cartilage pills, sold in 'health food' stores as a cancer preventative and treatment. By selling the pills as 'dietary supplements' rather than as medicine, the usual government controls requiring testing of new medical treatments were bypassed. The scientists conducting the research on which these products are based have publicly denounced them and denied that taking these pills could halt the progress of cancer. Controlled double-blind tests have shown that taking shark cartilage pills has no effect on the development of cancers in humans. In fact, sharks do suffer a remarkably low incidence of tumors, but this is due to their powerful immune systems, and is unrelated to their cartilaginous skeletons. Unidentified factors within cartilage (in all animals, not just sharks) do inhibit blood vessel growth, but these factors can apparently not be absorbed by ingesting the cartilage (just as insulin must be injected because it is digested if taken orally). Nonetheless, large numbers of desperate cancer victims and people fearful of coming down with this dreaded disease continue to purchase the pills. Some of those who spent their money on cartilage pills rather than proven medical treatments are now dead.

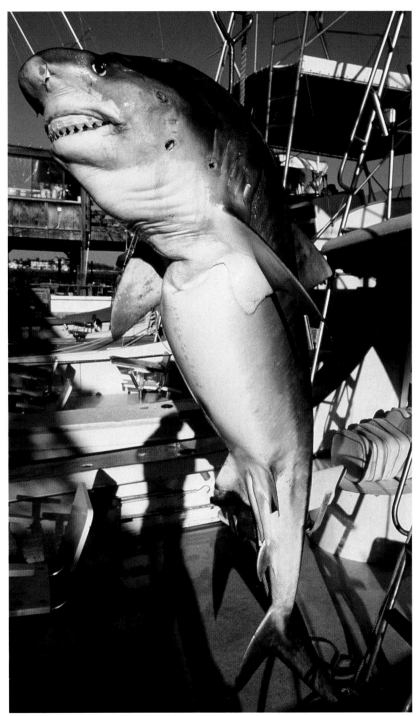

The fins above were cut from small sharks too young to reproduce, assuring that catches will continue to decline as the resource is depleted. The fins were photographed in a small, remote Caribbean village. There is no longer any location so remote that it has not been penetrated by fin buyers. The finned carcasses are sold for food, at a low price. By contrast, the only part of the tiger shark (right) that was used for any purpose was the teeth. Their sole use was to make jewelry. The rest of the carcass was discarded. For 'sport', the shark was hooked on a heavy line, dragged to the boat, and shot in the head before boating it to display the carcass.

In some areas, the added value of the cartilage, meat, or other products makes it worthwhile for fishers to bring shark carcasses back to shore for processing. However, in most of the world the fins are so much more valuable, and easy to store, than the rest of the shark, that fishers merely slice the fins off and dump the body back into the ocean. This is often done while the shark is still alive, leaving it

Blue shark (Prionace glauca) *killed by drift net.*

to die slowly from starvation and its injuries.

At the same time that prices for shark products were rising exponentially, rapid advances in boating and fishing technology were making it easier for fishers to work farther from shore. Very few populations of sharks or rays are still too remote to be exploited by modern fishing fleets. Incidental catches of elasmobranchs by fishers targeting other species may, however, be equal to or greater than the damage caused by directed fishing. Sharks and rays are not susceptible to most kinds of traditional fishing gear, which target much smaller fish. But the advent of longlines, purse seines, drift nets, and other modern fishing technologies has ensured that millions of sharks and rays will

die every year, even if they are not targeted. Longlines set for swordfish and tuna, for example, kill many times more sharks than either of the target species. Ironically, the dolphin-safe tuna campaign resulted in the deaths of countless numbers of sharks. When a purse seine is set on a pod of dolphin, the tuna associated with the dolphin are the only animals captured (unless a mistake is made and dolphin are killed). In order to qualify for the 'dolphin-safe' label, many boats switched to setting nets on floating logs and other debris. When a net is set around a floating object, it catches not only tuna, but also large numbers of sharks, sea turtles, other kinds of fish, and even sea birds.

Rays which rest on the bottom have no way to escape trawl nets that sweep the ocean floor for fish and shrimp. Shrimp trawls often catch many pounds of rays and skates for every pound of shrimp collected. Years of trawling have virtually eliminated some skates from entire ocean basins where they used to be both common and widespread. Ironically, the 'common skate', *Raja batis*, is now listed as endangered worldwide by the IUCN (International Union for the Conservation of Nature).

Trawls not only sweep up everything in their path, they also alter the ocean bottom itself. Flattening the sea floor reduces the number of hiding places for fish, and limits the number of fish that can live there, affecting rays and sharks, as well as other species. Although many people think of all sharks as spending their lives swimming endlessly in open ocean, many species have specific habitat requirements, and their survival is threatened by increasing destruction of those habitats. The most vulnerable are species that live in rivers or estuaries, such as river sharks, fresh water stingrays, and sawfish.

A number of requiem sharks which live well offshore as adults come into shallow estuaries to breed. These areas serve as nurseries for the pups. These habitats are rapidly being lost to development and pollution. Over half of the salt marshes and mangrove swamps in the United States were lost by the mid 1970s. Without breeding areas, populations are doomed. A particularly sad case concerns the lemon sharks of Bimini, Bahamas. Studies of this population over the last

20 years by Dr S.H. Gruber and colleagues at the University of Miami have formed the basis of much of what we know about the biology and behavior of requiem sharks. Gruber's studies established clearly that the mangroves fringing the lagoon are a critical habitat for newborn and juvenile sharks. As this book goes to press, plans have been announced to raze those mangroves (unnecessarily) for a resort and marina development.

Sad experience has taught us that without some form of regulation, levels of exploitation will usually exceed the capacity of fishery resources to regenerate themselves, and the fishery will collapse. Therefore, most economically important fisheries are managed by a variety of methods including closed seasons, size limits, catch limits, license requirements, limited entry, quotas, gear restrictions, closed areas, protection of reproductive aggregations, and so forth. Remarkably, very few elasmobranch fisheries have ever been managed in any way. Why have the same sort of rational controls applied to, for example, the collection of sea cucumbers, not been exercised with sharks and rays? Is it because they reproduce so prolifically that it would be impossible to catch enough to impact their populations?

In fact, the opposite is true. All elasmobranchs share life history characteristics that make them extremely susceptible to exploitation. Not only is the reproductive rate very low (as little as one offspring per year in some species), but it typically takes many years to reach the age of reproduction. Many bony fishes, by contrast, reach maturity in one to two years, and produce millions of eggs per year. In fisheries for these species, the number of young fish entering the fishery seems to depend primarily on environmental conditions which produce drastic variations in survival numbers of the many eggs spawned, and not so much on the numbers of adults producing the eggs. Therefore, in some cases, it has been possible to catch a high proportion of the adult fish each year without destroying the fishery. Yet, even for such prolific breeders as cod, enough fish were eventually taken to cause the population to collapse.

Shark fisheries have a history of crashing much more quickly. Sharks are naturally adapted to conditions of low natural mortality, and are among the longest-lived of any of the fishes. Therefore, a change to artificial conditions of high mortality often leads quickly to commercial extinction of a population, meaning that there are so few left that it is no longer worthwhile to fish for them. However, the gear used to catch sharks and rays is usually non-specific, so when one species is wiped out, fishers can continue to fish for the others, and catch the few remaining individuals of the species which are already over-exploited. Therefore some scientists believe that some types of sharks may be in danger of being driven into biological extinction – complete elimination of the organism from the earth.

The life history characteristics that make elasmobranchs so vulnerable – long lives, slow growth, large size, low rate of reproduction – are shared with some other groups of marine wildlife including whales, manatees, and sea turtles. When exploited heavily, populations of these animals have been severely reduced, and have generally recovered slowly, or not at all, even after complete protection. Phil Clapham, writing in his book, *Whales*, says that the 'whaling industry serves as a textbook case of how not to deal with an abundant but limited resource… its history embodies two common principles of mismanagement… The first is that, in the absence of certainty, the benefit of the doubt is almost always given to the exploiter rather than to the resource… The second… is that one can never demonstrate that a major problem would have actually occurred, had one not taken preventative measures [but] it is quite easy to demonstrate the economic consequences… that frequently accompany such prevention'.

These are the same two principles which are currently being used to justify stripping the oceans of sharks, in the same way that they were stripped of whales. Unfortunately sharks are not as 'cuddly', charismatic, or popular as whales, and are less likely to be saved by a public outcry. How many elasmobranchs are destroyed each year is impossible to know accurately. The near total lack of management includes a failure to compile catch records in most cases. The most widely used estimate is that around 100 million sharks have been caught per year over the last decade. The number of rays killed is unknown.

Sharks and rays are fished by over 100 nations. Of these, only 11 have any sort of management for elasmobranchs, and only four have integrated research and management programs. Even in these four, fishing restrictions have been inadequate, and too late to prevent the decline of most of the exploited populations. Many sharks migrate across national boundaries, or live offshore, in international waters. These populations require international management. However, the most suitable basis for such management, the United Nations Agreement on Straddling and Highly Migratory Fish Stocks, still needs (at this writing) to be ratified by 12 more countries before it comes into force. Another United Nations agreement, encouraging fishers to keep shark carcasses along with the fins, is also awaiting ratification as this book goes to press. Of the regional fishery management agencies that deal with migratory fishes such as tuna, in several parts of the world, none are actively managing elasmobranchs.

The Convention on International Trade in Endangered Species (CITES) prohibits its 133 member nations from importing or exporting wildlife products from species that are threatened with extinction. However, for the provisions to become effective, the species must be listed in the appendices to the treaty, by agreement of the member nations. Very few marine species have ever been listed. A movement to merely require member nations to start keeping records of elasmobranch catches was defeated at the 1987 meeting, primarily due to lobbying by the Japanese delegation.

The Convention on the Conservation of Migratory Species of Wild Animals ('Bonn Convention') likewise requires its 47 member states to conserve migratory species in danger of extinction. Like the CITES agreement, species must be listed in the appendices to receive protection. No commercially exploited marine species have been listed.

The Convention on Biological Diversity (CBD) requires its 133 members to adopt national strategies to maintain biodiversity. At the 1995 meeting, the members adopted the 'Jakarta Mandate on Marine and Coastal Biodiversity' encouraging members to implement policies promoting sustainable use of marine resources. As with the other two agreements, this has not yet resulted in any actual protection for over-exploited species of sharks and rays.

The result of continued inaction by regulatory agencies is that populations of a number of elasmobranch species are continuing to decline precipitously, and some species are actually facing extinction. Listed by the IUCN as endangered or critically endangered in at least parts of their ranges are sand tiger sharks, Ganges sharks, fresh water sawfish, smalltooth sawfish, largetooth sawfish, common sawfish, Brazilian guitarfish, common skates, and giant fresh water stingrays. Listed as vulnerable are great white sharks, porbeagles, and basking sharks.

What will be the consequences of greatly reduced numbers of sharks and rays in our oceans, and perhaps the complete elimination of some species? Nobody can say for sure. It is an 'experiment in progress'. Experts predict that the effects could be both far-reaching and unexpected. As apex predators, elasmobranchs influence the population dynamics of all the many species below them on the 'food pyramid' of the ocean. A great reduction in their numbers is bound to cause shifts in the ecosystem that will affect a great many other species. From a human perspective, the oceans will not be any safer, as all the major causes of death and injury will be unrelieved (drowning, sunburn, motorboats, surf, currents, etc.). However, the marine wilderness will be diminished in an unquantifiable way. An ocean without sharks and rays will be like the plains of Africa without lions and tigers, like the mountains of North America without wolves, or like the Arctic without polar bears. Yet another thread will be torn from the fabric of our world, reducing the magnificent tapestry of life by degrees to a ragged shawl.

Fortunately, in the last few years, some conservation groups have continued to try to prevent the extermination of sharks and their allies. Information is available from the sources listed on page 131.

Rays and skates are both killed deliberately for food, and captured incidentally in large numbers in bottom trawl fisheries. Generally, no records are kept of bycatch, which may be much larger than catches of target species, and populations can be nearly wiped out before scientists notice a problem.

The Classification of Sharks, Rays and Chimaeras

Classification systems change as new information and ideas emerge. Not all authorities agree on the same system. Common names vary.
The same common names may be used for different organisms which belong to different groups. Therefore you may see the same name listed under more than one family.

Class Chondrichthyes

SUBCLASS HOLOCEPHALI
Order Chimaeriformes
Family Callorhynchidae – elephant fishes
Family Rhinochimaeridae – spookfishes
Family Chimaeridae – shortnose chimaeras, ghost sharks

SUBCLASS ELASMOBRANCHII
Infraclass Euselachii
Cohort Neoselachii
Superorder Squalomorphi
Order Hexanchiformes
Suborder Chlamydoselachoidei
Family Chlamydoselachidae – frilled sharks
Suborder Hexanchoidei
Family Hexanchidae – sixgill and sevengill sharks
Order Squaliformes
Suborder Echinorhinoidei
Family Echinorhinidae – bramble sharks, prickly sharks
Suborder Squaloidei
Family Squalidae – dogfish sharks
Family Centrophoridae – gulper sharks
Family Etmopteridae – lantern sharks, velvet belly dogfish
Family Somniosidae – sleeper sharks, Greenland shark, velvet dogfish
Family Oxynotidae – rough sharks, prickly dogfish
Family Dalatiidae – kitefin sharks, cigar sharks, cookie-cutter sharks, pygmy sharks
Order Squatiniformes
Family Squatinidae – angel sharks, monkfish
Order Pristiophoriformes
Family Pristiophoridae – saw sharks
Order Rajiformes
Suborder Pristoidei
Family Pristidae – sawfishes
Suborder Rhinoidei
Family Rhinidae – bowmouth guitarfish
Suborder Rhynchobatoidei
Family Rhynchobatidae – shovelnose rays, sharkfin guitarfishes, shark rays, wedgefish
Suborder Torpedinoidei
Family Torpedinidae – torpedo rays
Family Hypnidae – coffin ray, short–tailed electric ray
Family Narcinidae – numbfish, electric rays
Family Narkidae – numbfish, shortnose electric rays, one-fin and finless electric rays
Suborder Rhinobatoidei
Family Rhinobatidae – guitarfish, violinfish, shovelnose rays, fiddler rays
Suborder Rajoidei
Family Arhynchobatidae – longtailed skate
Family Rajidae – skates, thornback rays
Family Anacanthobatidae – legskates
Suborder Platyrhinoidei
Family Platyrhinidae – thornback rays, fanrays

Suborder Zanobatoidei
Family Zanobatidae – striped thornback guitarfish, Atlantic roundhead guitarfish
Suborder Myliobatoidei
Family Plesiobatididae – giant stingaree
Family Hexatrygonidae – sixgill stingrays
Family Dasyatidae – stingrays
Family Urolophidae – round stingrays, stingarees
Family Urotrygonidae – round stingrays
Family Potamotrygonidae – fresh water stingrays
Family Gymnuridae – butterfly rays, diamond rays
Family Myliobatidae – eagle rays, bat rays, bullrays, duckbill rays
Family Rhinopteridae – cownose rays
Family Mobulidae – devil rays, mantas, mobulas

Superorder Galeomorphi
Order Heterodontiformes
Family Heterodontidae – horn sharks, bullhead sharks, Port Jackson sharks
Order Orectilobiformes
Family Parascylliidae – collared carpet sharks
Family Brachaeluridae – blind sharks
Family Orectilobidae – wobbegongs, carpet sharks
Family Hemiscylliidae – bamboo sharks, epaulette sharks
Family Pseudoginglymostomatidae – short-tail nurse shark
Family Stegostomatidae – zebra shark, leopard shark
Family Ginglymostomatidae – nurse sharks
Family Rhincodontidae – whale shark
Order Lamniformes
Family Carchariidae – sand tiger sharks
Family Odontaspididae – smalltooth and bigeye sand tiger sharks
Family Mitsukurinidae – goblin shark
Family Pseudocarcharidae – crocodile shark
Family Megachasmidae – megamouth shark
Family Alopiidae – thresher sharks
Family Cetorhinidae – basking shark
Family Lamnidae – mako, white, salmon, and porbeagle sharks
Order Carcharhiniformes
Family Scyliorhinidae – cat sharks, swell sharks, pyjama shark, shy sharks, puffadder shark
Family Proscylliidae – finback catsharks, ribbontail catsharks
Family Pseudotriakidae – false catsharks
Family Leptochariidae – barbeled houndsharks
Family Triakidae – hound sharks, smoothhounds, topes, whiskery sharks, gummy sharks, school shark, soupfin shark, leopard shark
Family Hemigaleidae – weasel sharks
Family Sphyrnidae – hammerhead sharks
Family Carcharhinidae – requiem sharks, whalers, gray sharks, reef sharks, tiger shark, spadenose shark, sandbar shark, dusky shark, brown shark, blacktip, silvertip, whitetip, spinner shark, silky shark, bull shark, Zambezi shark, Lake Nicaragua shark, blacknose shark, night shark, Galapagos shark, bignose shark, graceful shark, Ganges shark, blue shark, lemon sharks, milk shark, sharpnose sharks, etc.

Based on the Classification System of Dr L. J. V. Compagno.

Ordering the Orders

The chondrichthyans are a large and very diverse group of fishes. Exactly how large is impossible to say, because we have not yet discovered all the members of this class, many of which reside in the deep sea. New species are being discovered at the rate of about ten per year. In addition, scientists are not all in agreement about which slightly different forms should be considered separate species, and which should be classified only as subspecies or merely separate populations of the same species. The numbers which follow are estimates of the number of species known at the time of this writing. Because they include species which have not yet been scientifically described and named, these numbers are larger than those in the chapter, *What are Sharks and Rays?* By the time this book is printed they will be somewhat outdated, and as years go by, may begin to look like gross underestimates.

Chimaeras – 43 species;

Sharks – 465 species;

Rays – 627 species.

The division of the elasmobranchs into sharks and rays is an artificial separation, since most experts now believe that some groups of sharks are more closely allied with the rays than with the other groups of sharks. In this chapter we shall try to make some sense of the way that cartilaginous fishes are classified and take a closer look at a few sample species from each of the major groups.

To make some sense of the natural world, biologists try to place each type of organism within a hierarchical classification system with a discrete number of major divisions, and an infinite number of potential subdivisions. The classification system attempts to reflect the evolutionary origins of the organisms. It is always changing as we learn more about evolution and its historical path. Additionally, not all scientists agree on how to interpret the available information, so there are likely to be several different systems in competition at any one time.

At the highest level, there are divisions between various types of bacteria, other microbes, and the mitochondrial eukaryotes, which includes plants, fungi, and animals. Within the animal kingdom, the divisions, from largest to smallest, are: Phylum, Class, Order, Family, Genus, species. The *Genus* and *species* make up the two parts of the scientific name of any creature. However, nature is not as orderly as we would like, and animals do not all fall simply into groups with clear divisions between them. In order to better accommodate the continuity of evolution, all of these divisions can be subdivided further, or grouped together, into such categories as subclass, superorder, etc. When sub-, super-, and infra- prefixes do not suffice, additional terms such as 'cohort' and 'population' are added.

For the sake of simplicity, in this book we will consider divisions only to the level of orders. The system which will be followed is the one currently recommended by Dr Leonard J.V. Compagno, author of the widely used catalogues published by the Species Identification and Data Programme of the Food and Agriculture Organization (FAO) of the United Nations. It is somewhat different from the system previously used by Dr Compagno, which has been adopted in a number of popular books still in print. Differences between this system and those proposed by Dr Marcelo de Carvalho and Dr Shigeru Shirai, the other two most prominent authorities on the classification of elasmobranchs, are primarily of interest to scholars, but some comments based on Dr de Carvalho's analysis will be included.

The class Chondrichthyes, consisting of all the cartilaginous fishes, is divided into two subclasses: the Holocephali (chimaeras), and the Elasmobranchii (sharks and rays). The Holocephali consists of a single order, the Chimaeriformes. The divergence of the holocephalans, or chimaeras, from the sharks and rays occurred very early in the history of the Chondrichthyes. It has even been questioned whether these two groups are truly related, but most experts believe that they did have a common ancestor more than 400 MYA.

The Elasmobranchii is divided into two superorders, the Galeomorphi (or Galea) and the Squalomorphi (or Squalea). The Galeomorphi contains four orders of sharks: Heterodontiformes; Orectilobiformes; Lamniformes; and Carcharhiniformes. The Squalomorphi contains four orders of sharks, and one of rays: Hexanchiformes; Squaliformes; Squatiniformes; Pristiophoriformes; and Rajiformes (or Batoidea). All of the orders within each superorder are considered to be more closely related to each other than to any of the orders in the other superorder.

The list of orders below will not mention all of the criteria that are used by specialists to define one group as separate from another (most of these depend on fairly obscure features of the internal anatomy). Instead we'll list some of the more apparent features that are common within an order, and some common names of animals that belong to the order. Space constraints only allow a detailed look at a few of the more than 1000 species of cartilaginous fishes. For detailed information on all the known species of elasmobranchs, and classification into families, the reader is referred to the FAO species catalogues.

Order Chimaeriformes

Contains three families with 36 species of fishes known variously as chimaeras, ratfish, rattails, ghost sharks, rabbitfish, elephantfish, and spookfish. These are primarily deep-water fishes, although, in temperate zones, a few are found shallow enough to be encountered by divers. They have smooth skin, without scales, with a metallic sheen in some species. The tail is long and tapered (hence the name ratfish). The teeth are in solid plates. The first dorsal fin is retractable. The head is crossed with mucus canals associated with the lateral line system. Reproduction is by deposition of egg cases on the bottom. Males have pelvic, pre-pelvic, and frontal (head) claspers.

SPECIES SNAPSHOT: Spotted Ratfish, *Hydrolagus colliei*; Family Chimaeridae
The spotted ratfish is found along the west coast of North America,

from Alaska at least as far south as Baja California. It is most common from British Columbia to northern California. It inhabits waters from the surface down to at least 3000 ft (900 m). It is commonly found in depths of 16–330 ft (5–100 m) in the northern part of its range, tending to move into shallower water at night, but occurs deeper in the southern part, where surface waters are warm. The body is dark with white spots and an elongated flattened snout. The thin tail provides little propulsion, so the large pectoral fins are flapped like wings during swimming. It spends most of its time on, or close to, the bottom, usually in sand or mud, and feeds primarily on benthic (bottom-dwelling) invertebrates, including shrimps, snails, urchins, worms, and crabs, but also eats some bottom-dwelling fish, including its own kind. The foredorsal spine is mildly venomous.

Order Heterodontiformes

Contains one family with nine species known as horn sharks, bullhead sharks, and Port Jackson sharks. These are bottom-dwelling sharks with a large squarish head and a crest above each eye. In juveniles, all teeth are sharp and multi-cusped, but in adults the rear teeth are molar-like. The diet consists of benthic invertebrates and small fish. The two dorsal fins are large, and each carries a defensive spine in front. The pectoral fins are also large, and are used for walking on the bottom. As in all of the Galeomorphi, there is an anal fin, and five gill slits. The distinctive egg cases have an auger-like ridge spiraling around them.

SPECIES SNAPSHOT: Crested Bullhead Shark, *Heterodontus galeatus*;
Family Heterodontidae
The crested bullhead shark, or crested Port Jackson shark, is found along the east coast of Australia, in southern Queensland and New South Wales. The crests over the eyes are higher and more prominent than in any other horn shark. The color is brown with dark saddles behind each dorsal, a dark band below the first dorsal, and dark wedges under each eye and on the nape. The distinctive harness-like pattern found on the related Port Jackson shark is not present.

The crested bullhead shark (Heterodontus galeatus) is so named due to the high crests over the eyes. Bullhead sharks are also known as horn sharks because of the spines in front of the dorsal fins, and are sometimes referred to as Port Jackson sharks, after one of the better-known species.

*The presence of whale sharks (Rhincodon typus) in clear plankton-free tropical
waters, such as this one off the coast of Hawaii, can be explained by the fact that deep-water
plankton migrates upward at night, enabling the shark to feed on plankton by night.*

Crested bullhead sharks are found from the shoreline to depths of about 300 ft (90 m). They feed primarily on sea urchins, which often stain their teeth purple, but also eat other shellfish, and small fishes. Like their more common relatives, the Port Jackson sharks, they probably hunt mostly by smell. The rear teeth are shaped like paving stones, and are used for crushing hard-shelled prey. The forward teeth are small and sharp, and multi-cuspid in juveniles, with a shape like a maple leaf.

The egg cases have tendrils at one end which help to anchor them when they are deposited in algae or sponges. They are laid in July–August, and hatch after about 5 to 8 months. The pups hatch at a size of about 7–9 in (17–22 cm), and grow to a maximum length of 4–5 ft (1.2–1.5m).

The sharp spines in front of both dorsal fins serve as an effective defense against most predators. There is no commercial fishery for this species, but they are sometimes captured in bottom trawls. Horn sharks pose no hazard to humans, but can bite if provoked.

Order Orectilobiformes

Contains seven families with a total of 34 species known as wobbegongs, carpet sharks, blind sharks, nurse sharks, bamboo sharks, epaulette sharks, whale sharks, and zebra sharks. These are predominantly bottom-dwelling sharks, with the notable exception of the whale shark, which can be presumed (by its appearance) to have adopted its pelagic habits in relatively recent evolutionary history. The head tends to be squarish or flattened, not pointed, and there are barbels at the inside edges of the nostrils. In most species, the nostrils are connected by grooves to the mouth, enabling the shark to pump water across its nostrils while resting on the bottom, making it possible to sample the water for food odors without swimming. The mouth is well forward of the eyes. There are two dorsal fins, without spines, one anal fin, and five gill slits. The order includes both egg-laying and live-bearing species. They feed on bottom-dwelling invertebrates and fish, except for the whale shark, which feeds on plankton and small schooling fish.

SPECIES PROFILE: Whale Shark, *Rhincodon typus*; Family Rhincodontidae
The whale shark is the largest fish in the world. How large they get, nobody knows. The largest one accurately measured was 40 ft (12.1 m), but there are many reports of sightings of much larger animals. They may grow to 60 ft (18 m). The blocky body, flattened head and underside, and large spiracle give the appearance of a bottom-dwelling shark, from which they may have evolved, but the nearly symmetrical caudal (tail) fin and pre-caudal keel are obvious adaptations for the pelagic existence that they have adopted. Apart from the size and odd shape, they are distinguished by ridges running down the length of the body, and a color pattern of white polka dots, bands, and stripes on a gray background, creating the appearance of a giant game board.

Whale sharks are found around the world in a broad band on both sides of the equator. Some undertake extensive travels, which we are just beginning to learn about through satellite tagging. One that was tagged in the Sea of Cortez, in Mexico, was tracked 8000 miles (13,000 km) to the Marshall Islands, in the central Pacific, over a three-year period. They are able to locate seasonal food sources, with aggregations appearing in certain locations year after year. They are often seen at or near the surface, but are capable of diving to at least 800 ft (240 m). They seem to prefer areas with warm surface waters close to upwellings of cooler water which bring up nutrients that stimulate plankton production. Whale sharks feed both by gulping or pumping in prey, and by merely swimming through the water with the mouth open and filtering out plankton by means of a unique sieve-like structure on the inside of the gill rakers. Food items include small crustaceans and other plankton and possibly small schooling fishes. The primary food source seems to be organisms in the 0.08–0.15 in (2–4 mm) size range. They are often seen swimming through schools of fish with open mouths, but may merely be feeding on the same plankton as the fish. There are about 300 rows of tiny hooked teeth in each jaw, which are apparently completely non-functional.

They are non-aggressive towards humans, and sometimes curious or even playful. The mouth can be large enough to take in a person, theoretically. This has led to speculation about possible origins of the Jonah story, but the opening to the throat would not allow passage of anything larger than a fist. The reproductive mode was uncertain until 1995. An egg case dredged up from the ocean floor had previously led some researchers to believe that this species was an egg-layer. But in 1995, a 35 ft (10.5 m) female was found with 307 embryos inside, from 16–25 in (41–64 cm) in length, proving that the egg cases hatch within the mother. This is by far the largest number of offspring recorded from any cartilaginous fish, but may even be a low number for the species, since whale sharks grow much larger.

In spite of the high reproductive rate (for sharks), whale sharks are considered to be in peril, with numbers apparently dwindling around the world. Possible causes include direct fishing by humans, entanglement in fishing nets, collisions with motor vessels, and environmental changes. A harpoon fishery was recently banned in the Philippines, but fisheries still exist in India and Taiwan, where a single whale shark is reported to be worth U.S. $20,000. Other enemies include orcas, which attack in groups and can completely butcher a whale shark, and sharks, which can eat a small whale shark, or bite pieces off a larger one. A whole newborn whale shark, 1½ ft (58 cm) long, was once found in the stomach of a blue shark. When threatened, a whale shark turns its back (where the skin is thickest) towards the source of the threat. Whale sharks are officially protected in the Maldives, the Philippines, Western Australia, Israel, and along the Atlantic and Gulf coasts of the U.S.A.

SPECIES SNAPSHOT: Epaulette Shark, *Hemiscyllium ocellatum*;
Family Hemiscylliidae
The epaulette shark is a member of the bamboo shark family, also known as longtail carpet sharks or banded cat sharks. It occurs along the coast of the northern half of Australia, plus the entire coast of the island of New Guinea. It is a small shark, reaching just over 3 ft (1 m) in length. The body is slender, tapering to a long tail with no lower lobe. The color is an attractive tan with small dark spots and a large

black ocellus, or false eye, ringed in white, just above and behind each pectoral fin. (This is the 'epaulette' from which the common name is derived.) There is a large spiracle just behind and below the eye.

Epaulette sharks are fairly common on shallow coral reefs within their range, especially on the Great Barrier Reef, and can be found from tidepools to a depth of about 33 ft (10 m). They are most active at night, but can sometimes be seen during the day. They clamber about the bottom feeding on small benthic invertebrates which they either dig out of the sand, or suck out of crevices in the coral. The short barbels are probably used to detect the hidden prey. The teeth are small and pointed, with a triangular cusp. The paired fins are used almost like legs when 'walking' on the bottom. Epaulette sharks are even capable of walking on land, although they can't breathe out of the water. This skill might help them get from one tidepool to another on very low tides.

The sticky ellipsoidal egg cases are laid at night, two at a time, and hatch about four months later. In captivity about 50 eggs are laid per year. The pups hatch at about 6 in (15 cm).

The only fishery for epaulette sharks is live capture for the aquarium trade. They will bite if provoked, but are generally considered harmless.

Order Lamniformes
Contains eight families with 17 species, including great white sharks, mako sharks, porbeagles, threshers, basking sharks, sand tigers, crocodile sharks, goblin sharks, and megamouths. Collectively known as 'mackerel sharks', they have long snouts with a mouth that reaches behind the eyes. There are two dorsal fins, without spines, one anal fin, and five gill slits. This and the order Carcharhiniformes ('ground sharks') contain most of the 'shark-like' sharks. Unlike the ground sharks, there is no nictitating membrane to protect the eye, and instead of a spiral or scroll valve in the intestine, there is a ring valve. Reproduction is live-bearing with no placenta, with the unique twist that embryos nourish themselves within the uterus by consuming eggs and sometimes other embryos as well.

The pelagic thresher (top left) belongs to the same order as white sharks, makos, and megamouths. The long tails of threshers are used like whips in feeding. The epaulette shark (top right) is a small bottom-dwelling bamboo, named for its black 'shoulder spot'. The spotted ratfish (bottom left) is a chimaera, not a true shark or ray. The great hammerhead (bottom right) has a taller dorsal fin than other members of the hammerhead family. It is also distinguished by a straight forward margin on the head.

SPECIES PROFILE: Great White Shark, *Carcharodon carcharias*; Family Lamnidae

The white shark has a white belly, like most other sharks, but is dark gray on top. The conical snout gives it the name 'white pointer' in Australia. The eye is so dark that the pupil is not distinguishable, giving the eye the appearance of a black hole. During feeding, the eye is rolled back into the socket for protection. The first dorsal fin is large, and the second very small. The pectoral fins are tipped in black on the underside, and sometimes have a black spot at the axil. The caudal (tail) fin is nearly symmetrical – built for speed and long-distance cruising. The gill slits are very long. The serrated teeth are similar in both jaws in adults – large and triangular, for sawing apart large prey such as seals and sea lions. In juveniles, the lower teeth are more slender and pointed – a better design for catching and holding fish.

Prey includes a wide variety of bony fish, sharks, rays, seals, sea lions, dolphins, crabs, abalone and other invertebrates, carrion, and occasionally turtles and birds. Sharks larger than 10 ft (3 m) prefer marine mammals, whereas smaller ones feed predominantly on fish. Large white sharks sometimes attack humans, sea otters, boats, floats, and other items not normally found in their diet. Otters are commonly killed, but have not been found in stomach contents. Seabirds, especially penguins, are also regularly attacked, but not consumed. Human victims are killed in only about one quarter of white shark attacks, and even less frequently eaten. Some researchers believe that white sharks strike unfamiliar objects in order to test them as potential food sources. Items such as humans, otters, birds, surfboards, etc. which have a low fat content are rejected. It takes days for a large meal to pass through a shark's digestive system, and eating one of these unsuitable items would hinder the shark from feeding on a calorie-rich, high-fat seal, sea lion, or tuna fish. An alternative theory is that white sharks make an initial strike, then release their prey and wait for it to bleed to death, to avoid injury by the struggling prey. Recent research in California has cast some doubt on this theory, but neither proposal has been proven or disproven. Yet other ideas include suggestions that white shark attacks may constitute 'play' or 'target practice'.

White sharks are found worldwide in temperate and tropical waters, but are much more common in temperate zones, especially near colonies of seals and sea lions. The highest concentrations appear to be in South Australia, South Africa, and central California. They seem to prefer waters in the range of about 57–72°F (14–22°C). Larger sharks appear to have a greater tolerance for both high and low water temperatures. Blood vessels which function as a counter-current heat exchanger warm the eyes, brain, muscles, and digestive system of white sharks, enabling them to maintain a high level of metabolism and activity even in very cool waters. White sharks can maintain internal temperatures at least 24.7°F (13.7°C) above the temperature of the surrounding water, and may be able to regulate their body temperature at a fairly constant level. Although most sharks that live in cool water appear to be fairly sluggish, white sharks are active predators, and may have a metabolic rate close to that of mammals and birds. They occasionally breach entirely out of the water.

White sharks hatch from egg cases within the mother, and feed on infertile eggs until they are born at a length of 4–5 ft (1.2–1.5 m). The few pregnant white sharks that have been captured were carrying 4 to 14 embryos. At birth they are fully developed with functional teeth, and ready to live on their own, but cannot tolerate waters as cold as an adult can. In California it appears that pregnant white sharks migrate south to give birth in warmer water, and adults migrate north to feed in cooler, richer waters. Males and females often occupy separate areas. When and where mating occurs is not known. Females are estimated to mature at an age of 9 to 10 years.

Because of the difficulties in studying white sharks, estimates of population sizes are hard to come by, but it appears that they have never been large, and have been reduced by sport fishing, trophy hunting,

Most great white sharks are counter-shaded, dark above and white below. However large individuals are often pale, as suggested by the name.

'revenge' killings, shark control programs, and incidental catches in commercial fisheries. White sharks are listed as 'vulnerable' by the IUCN (International Union for the Conservation of Nature). The species has recently been protected in South Africa, Australia, California, the Atlantic and Gulf coasts of the United States, the Maldives, Israel, and Namibia.

SPECIES SNAPSHOT: Pelagic Thresher Shark, *Alopias pelagicus*;
Family Alopiidae

The pelagic thresher is one of three or possibly four species of thresher sharks, which are distinguished by an extremely asymmetrical tail, with a scythe-shaped upper lobe which is as long, or nearly as long, as the rest of the body. The tail is used almost like a scythe or whip, to chop through schools of fish and squid, herding and stunning or killing the prey before feeding. They have long pectoral fins, a large first dorsal and small second dorsal, a small anal fin, short gill slits, and small blade-like teeth with cusplets. They are slightly smaller than common and bigeye threshers, and have smaller eyes. The maximum length is about 11 ft (3.3 m), including the tail.

Pelagic threshers inhabit tropical oceanic waters from the west coast of the Americas to the Red Sea and the east coast of Africa. They are usually found in offshore, near-surface waters, but are occasionally seen close to land, and occur from the surface to depths of at least 500 ft (152 m). They have been seen approaching coral drop-offs on oceanic islands to utilize the services of cleaner fishes.

Pelagic threshers are believed to be partly or fully warm-bodied, as are the bigeye and common threshers. Females are able to bear pups after they reach a size of about 8½ ft (2.6 m). Usually only two pups are born per litter, after eating the other eggs and possibly embryos as well. They are almost 3 ft (1 m) in length when born. They have been exploited for meat, vitamin A (from the liver), leather, and fins. They are considered harmless to humans.

SPECIES PROFILE: Megamouth Shark, *Megachasma pelagios*;
Family Megachasmidae

The megamouth shark is a living reminder that the sea has yet to give up all of its mysteries. The existence of such a huge, bizarre creature was not even suspected until 1976 when one became tangled in some lines deployed beneath a research vessel. It was found to be not only a new species, but also a new genus, and a new family, with only distant ties to the other mackerel sharks. It is not closely related to anything known to science! At the time of this writing, a total of 12 specimens have been captured, on both sides of the Atlantic and Pacific, as well as the Indian Ocean, in both tropical and temperate zones. Six of these have been preserved at museums or other institutions, three were discarded, two released alive, and one was chopped up and eaten in the village where it was captured. One of the released sharks (No. 6) was tagged with a transmitter and tracked for two days, giving us the only meager bit of information that we have about the natural behavior of this species. A thirteenth megamouth was photographed at the surface, but not captured. When sighted, it was in the company of three sperm whales, which appeared to be attacking the shark.

The largest megamouth taken was about 18 ft (5.5 m) in length. There are two dorsal fins, the second much smaller than the first, a small anal fin, long narrow pectoral fins, and a caudal fin with the upper lobe much larger than the lower. The body is flabby, and, as the name implies, the mouth is enormous – over 3 ft (1 m) in width. It has a silvery lining in the mouth and an unusual white 'mustache' above the upper 'lip'. The function of these markings is uncertain, but scientists have speculated that the silver lining may serve to reflect light generated by planktonic organisms, and attract more prey. The 'mustache', which can only be seen when the upper jaw is thrust forward, might be flashed to communicate social signals, perhaps during courtship, or as a threat display.

The primary food is krill and other small crustaceans, which are filtered from the water as the shark swims slowly forward with an

Megamouth sharks eat only tiny plankton, and do not use their small hooked teeth in feeding. The teeth may be used only in courtship and mating.

Basking sharks, like sperm whales, whale sharks, and megamouth sharks, have a reflective lining
inside the mouth. Scientists speculate that such color patterns may serve to attract prey into the mouth.
However, the prey of basking sharks consists of tiny organisms with somewhat limited mobility.

open mouth. The megamouth that was tracked cruised at a slow speed of about 1 mph (1.5–2 km/hr). By day it stayed deep, at about 500 ft (150 m), but still well above the bottom. At nightfall it ascended to a depth of about 56 ft (17 m) and leveled off, returning to the depths again at first light. This is the same daily vertical migration pattern followed by krill. It appeared that the shark was adjusting its depth to stay at a constant light level. The more than 100 rows of tiny hook-like teeth are not used for feeding, but may be used by the males to grasp females during mating.

One intriguing thing that was learned from megamouth No. 6 during its live captivity is that respiration is accomplished by pumping water over the gills, so that the shark does not have to keep swimming in order to breathe. In fact, during its captivity, the megamouth spent long periods resting on the bottom. This is completely unexpected for a shark that is presumed to be entirely pelagic, spending its whole life swimming constantly in the open ocean. Is it possible that megamouth sharks rest on the bottom when plankton is in short supply? Or do they perhaps just float in mid water when not feeding? It could be that the ability to pump water over the gills is merely retained from a recent shallow-water ancestor. The color of the living megamouth has been described as a 'golden bronze' countershaded with a white belly – a color pattern more typical of shallow-water sharks than of deep-sea fishes.

Details of reproduction and most other aspects of the natural history of megamouths remain unknown. There are no fisheries for them, and they pose no threat to humans.

SPECIES PROFILE: Basking Shark, *Cetorhinus maximus*; Family Cetorhinidae
The basking shark is the second-largest fish in the sea (after the whale shark), and one of only three types of sharks that are filter feeders (with megamouth and whale sharks). In spite of the fact that it is large, occurs in temperate-boreal waters around the world, feeds right at the surface and often close to the coast, has been the subject of commercial fisheries, and is regularly taken as bycatch in other fisheries, we know little more about the life of this strange animal than we do about the mysterious megamouth.

Basking sharks are born at an estimated 5–6½ ft (1.5–2 m), the largest size at birth of any known elasmobranch. They reach a maximum size of perhaps 45 ft (14 m), but most are 33 ft (10 m) or less in length. A 30 ft (9 m) specimen weighed 8600 lb (3900 kg). The color can vary from dark blue to gray to brown. The second dorsal fin is about the size of the anal fin, while the first is more than twice as large. The caudal fin is nearly symmetrical. The gill slits are extremely long, wrapping almost completely around the head. A narrow conical snout positioned above a huge yawning mouth and buttonlike round eyes give this harmless animal a comical appearance, as if gaping in astonishment, that cannot help but endear it to the viewer. In small juveniles the snout is elongated to the point that it looks like a short trunk with a hooked end. It is believed to assist somehow in juvenile feeding, perhaps even within the womb.

Male basking sharks mature at 13–16 ft (4–5 m), but females do not reach maturity until they are 26–32 ft (8–10 m) long, at an estimated age of 20 years. Amazingly, scientists have never examined a pregnant female, so nothing is known of the reproductive system, although it is assumed to be similar to that of other lamniform sharks. Only one pregnant basking shark has ever been reported, and it was carrying five very large pups. Gestation is thought to last over a year, and possibly up to three-and-a-half years. Basking sharks are found singly, in small groups, and in schools of up to a hundred or more. These groups are usually segregated by sex and size. In the British fishery, 40 females were captured for every male during the summer. In the winter very few sharks were caught, but they were mostly males.

Basking sharks are believed to be responsible for numerous sightings of sea serpents, for two reasons. While feeding, they often swim at the surface with dorsal and caudal fins protruding from the water, in lines of three or more sharks, which may appear like the undulating body of a giant serpent. Secondly, decomposition reduces the stocky body of a basking shark to a narrow skeleton, which bears little resemblance to the live shark.

One of the most amazing characteristics of basking sharks is their ability to leap entirely clear of the water, possibly in attempts to dislodge lampreys or other parasites. This is a remarkable feat for an animal weighing several tons. Their struggles when harpooned also show them to be powerful animals, in spite of their lethargic cruising pace of about 2 knots when feeding.

Basking sharks feed on minute crustaceans (mostly copepods, and some barnacle and crab larvae), and fish eggs, which they filter out with their giant gill rakers. They are estimated to filter over 2000 tons of water per hour through a mouth that can stretch over 3 ft (1 m) across, and average half a ton of food in the stomach at a time. They have an uncanny ability to locate plankton blooms, even when the plankton occurs in small patches. How they locate these is not known. Nor is it known how they manage to select patches which are rich in the particular species of large copepods they prefer. In winter, when copepods are no longer available in abundance, the sharks shed their gill rakers and disappear. No one knows where they go, but it has been hypothesized that they sink to the bottom of the ocean and hibernate for 4 to 5 months, then re-grow their gill rakers before beginning to feed again in the spring. Alternatively, it has been suggested that they may feed on bottom-dwelling organisms during the winter, or cruise slowly in the depths, subsisting off the energy stores in their liver oil.

The skin of basking sharks is unique in being covered with a thick, black, foul-smelling mucus, and also in that the dermal denticles point in all directions, rather than all pointing towards the tail, as in other elasmobranchs. Thus the skin of the basking shark is rough when touched from any direction, and is likely to produce abrasion injuries if a swimmer gets in the path of the shark and is bumped. Other than that, they pose no threat to humans, except when attacked. They have over 200 rows of tiny hook-like teeth, which are not used in feeding, but apparently come into play during courtship and mating, judging from scars seen on females.

The enormous liver of the basking shark fills up a large part of the body cavity, and contains up to 600 gallons (2300 liters) of oil, providing both flotation and energy reserves to the shark. The oil was considered to be of high quality, nearly equal to that of sperm whale oil, in the days when most lamps and streetlights burned oil, and the Yankee whalers took basking sharks as well as whales. The oil is also a source of vitamin A, and has been used to extract experimental anti-cancer remedies. Basking sharks have been hunted for oil, meat, fish meal for fertilizer and animal feed, leather, and fins, off the north-east and west coasts of North America, Norway, Iceland, Ireland, the Orkneys, Japan, Ecuador and Peru. Most fisheries collapsed due to overfishing and instability of prices for the products. An eradication program was conducted in British Columbia in the 1950s by the Canadian Fisheries Department because basking sharks were damaging salmon nets when they became accidentally entangled. The sharks were killed by ramming them with a sharp, pointed device attached to the front of a boat. In most of the world, basking shark populations have declined to the point where it is not economical to fish them, but a fin fishery persists in Norway and they continue to be killed by entanglement in salmon nets, drift gillnets, and other fishing devices. Their habit of feeding right at the surface also makes them vulnerable to collisions with motor vessels, and to deliberate harassment. A few modest ecotourism operations take customers to view basking sharks in the United Kingdom. They are officially ranked as vulnerable, due to a lack of information which precludes designating an 'endangered' status. Basking sharks are protected in Great Britain, Israel, along the Atlantic and Gulf coasts of the United States, and in New Zealand.

Order Carcharhiniformes

Contains eight families with 259 species, known as requiem sharks, whalers, reef sharks, cat sharks, swell sharks, draughtsboard sharks, hound sharks, weasel sharks, soupfin or tope sharks, leopard sharks, and

The shortfin mako shark (Isurus oxyrhinchus) *is a mackerel shark. The similar longfin mako shark is less common.*

hammerheads. Collectively, they are sometimes called 'ground sharks'. The family Carcharhinidae, or requiem sharks, includes many of the familiar 'shark-like' sharks, such as the blacktip, whitetip and silvertip sharks, tiger shark, lemon shark, blue shark, bull shark, gray reef shark, Caribbean reef shark, bronze whaler, silky shark, sandbar shark, and Galapagos shark. Ground sharks have five gill slits, a long mouth that reaches behind the eyes, an anal fin, two dorsal fins with no spines, a spiral or scroll valve in the intestine, and a unique semi-transparent 'third eyelid' called a nictitating membrane, which comes up from beneath to protect the eye while feeding. They have a variety of tooth types, but none have large crushing teeth at the back like the Heterodontiformes. Some are egg-layers, and others are live-bearers (both with placentas and without). Ground sharks inhabit both tropical and cold seas, and are found in fresh water as well. They are the most abundant order of sharks, in both numbers of species and numbers of individuals.

SPECIES PROFILE: Great Hammerhead Shark, *Sphyrna mokarran*;
Family Sphyrnidae

The great hammerhead is the largest of nine known species in the hammerhead family. This is one of the most recently evolved shark families, and is distinguished by the extended lateral head lobes. These are considered to be an advanced feature, for which several functions have been proposed. The wide placement of the nostrils at the ends of the lobes may improve the ability to track scent gradients. There may also be some expansion of the visual field by the placement of the eyes at the ends of the lobes, but this is harder to conceptualize, and some divers have reported that hammerheads appear to have a 'blind spot' directly in front of them, for which they can compensate only by swinging the head in a broad arc as they swim. The broad head may also serve as an expanded surface for the placement of electrosense organs. This is supported by observations of hammerheads swinging their heads just over the surface of the sand in a motion reminiscent of a person operating a metal detector. Stingrays, which are one of the preferred food sources of great hammerheads, often bury themselves in the sand, so an enhanced electrosense would certainly be adaptive in food gathering. It has also been hypothesized that the broad head forms an expanded planing surface, providing hydrodynamic lift to compensate for the heavy body (one of the most negatively buoyant of all sharks), and the small pectoral fins. As a corollary, it has been suggested that the head shape improves maneuverability. This is reinforced by an observation of a great hammerhead using its head like a braking fin to make a sudden dive and pin a stingray against the bottom before consuming it. The hammerhead was also able to use its flat rostrum to hold the ray down more effectively than a shark with a normal conical snout could have.

Hammerheads have five short gill slits, an asymmetrical tail, with the upper lobe more than twice the length of the lower, moderately large anal and second dorsal fins, and a larger first dorsal fin. The great hammerhead is distinguished by an extremely high first dorsal, which appears disproportionate to the rest of the body, and a nearly straight margin at the front of the head. It is born at a length of 20–28 in (50–70 cm) and attains a maximum length of about 20 ft (6 m), although most adults are not more than 12 ft (3.7 m). The color is gray or brown above, and light below, with no fin markings.

Great hammerheads are found in tropical waters around the world, both around islands and along continental coasts and shelves from close to shore to well out to sea, and from the surface down to at least 260 ft (80 m). Individuals have been reported to be resident in some areas for years, but others appear to be nomadic or to have seasonal migrations. They are usually solitary, and are not known to school, as does the scalloped hammerhead.

Like all hammerheads, they are placental live-bearers. Females mature at a length of 8–9 ft (2.5–3 m) and bear 6 to 42 pups in a litter. The gestation period is believed to be about 11 months.

*The zebra shark of the Indo-West Pacific (*Stegostoma fasciatum*) not to be confused with that of the eastern North Pacific (*Triakis semifasciata*).*

Great hammerheads feed on a variety of fish and invertebrates, but seem to prefer elasmobranchs. One 15 ft (4.5 m) specimen in the Bahamas had a 9 ft (2.7 m) lemon shark in its stomach. They do not seem to be deterred by the spines of catfish or stingrays. One individual had 96 stingray barbs in its mouth, throat, and tongue. They also seem unfazed by the poisons found in trunkfishes and pufferfishes, which can be deadly to other fishes, and to humans. They have a reputation of being dangerous to humans, in contrast to the other members of the hammerhead family, which are considered harmless. Actual attacks on humans have not been verified, but this species is known to harass spear-fishers. Considering their demonstrated ability to swallow large sharks whole, they should probably be treated with some caution.

Great hammerheads are fished throughout their range for meat, leather, cartilage, fins, oil, and fishmeal, and for sport and trophies. They are also killed in shark control nets. The conservation status of this species is unknown, and there is little to no information available about population sizes or parameters.

SPECIES SNAPSHOT: Swell Shark, *Cephaloscyllium ventriosum*;
Family Scyliorhinidae

The swell shark is a small (maximum length about 3 ft [1 m]) bottom-dwelling cat shark found along the west coast of North and South America, from California to Mexico, and off central Chile, from the coastline to a depth of about 1500 ft (450 m). It is active by night, and rests in caves and crevices by day, sometimes with other individuals which may pile on top of each other. Its common name derives from its ability to inflate its stomach with water (or air if removed from the water) up to three times the normal size, as a protection against predation. It can increase its size this way to make it more difficult to swallow, or can use the same trick to wedge itself into a crevice so tightly that it is impossible to remove. The body is tan to brown, with dark and light bands running across it, punctuated by light and dark spots of various sizes. Large nasal flaps reach down to the mouth. The two rounded dorsal fins are both placed far back towards the tail, with the first dorsal over the pelvic fins, and the second over the anal fins.

Swell sharks feed on bony fishes and crustaceans. Schooling fish, such as blacksmith, are captured by ambush. The swell shark lies quietly on the bottom, in the dark, until one of the fish ventures too close, then suddenly engulfs it. The teeth are small, but dagger-like and multi-cuspid, well-adapted for holding large fish.

Eggs are laid on the bottom in large, amber to green, purse-shaped cases, with tendrils. The pups hatch out in 7½ to 10 months depending on water temperature, at a length of 5–6 in (13–15 cm). They have special spines in a double row down the back, which they use to ratchet themselves out of the egg case. The spines disappear soon after hatching.

Swell sharks can bite if sufficiently provoked but are normally docile and present no danger to humans. There is no fishery for them, but populations in California have declined in areas where they were once common, possibly due to changing water temperatures, or loss of kelp and algae beds, which they prefer.

SPECIES PROFILE: Tiger Shark, *Galeocerdo cuvier*; Family Carcharhinidae

The tiger shark is an unmistakable large requiem shark, which is found around the world in both tropical and temperate seas, from the shoreline, and in estuaries, to far out to sea, and from the surface to a depth of at least 1150 ft (350 m). It has a big squarish head, with large sad-looking eyes, which often show a dark 'drip' mark extending from the pupil to the bottom of the eye. Pups are born with a 'jaguar' pattern of dark gray spots on a silvery gray background. As they grow, the spots coalesce into a striped pattern of bars and blotches. In older individuals the pattern fades, leaving a uniformly gray upper surface. The underside is white to cream-colored at all ages. The tail is asymmetrical, with the upper lobe longer than the lower, and notched towards the tip. The second dorsal is similar to the moderately sized

Swell sharks are members of the cat shark family which have the ability to swell themselves up to avoid being eaten by larger sharks, fish, or mammals.

anal fin, with a much larger first dorsal. The teeth are deeply serrated, and have a unique notched and angled shape.

Tiger sharks are born at a length of about 20–35 in (50–90 cm), and may grow as long as 24 ft (7.4 m), but few surpass 16 ft (5 m). The lifespan is estimated to be about 50 years. Females mature at a length of 8–12 ft (2.5–3.5 m) at an age of 8 to 10 years. They probably reproduce only every other year, bearing 6 to 82 pups after a gestation period of a year or more. Tigers bear their young alive, like all requiem sharks, but do not have a placenta, as do the rest of the family. They may nourish the embryos by uterine secretions, as well as from the egg yolk. Females are able to store sperm after mating and use it later to fertilize eggs.

The feeding habits of tiger sharks defy categorization. Many of them appear to move into shallow nearshore waters to feed at night, and retire to deeper waters by day, but they have also been seen feeding by day on numerous occasions. Studies in Hawaii indicate that they have very large feeding ranges. They travel long distances from one part of their range to another, and may return to a specific site at infrequent intervals. In summer they may move into high latitudes, retreating to the tropics in the winter. They are often observed to be very cautious feeders, approaching potential food sources slowly, and circling and/or bumping the item for long periods before attempting to feed on it. At times, nonetheless, they are reported to attack at high speed without warning. Tiger sharks appear to be solitary by nature, and do not school, but more than a dozen may appear at a time to feed on a whale carcass. In such situations, they take turns feeding and appear to observe a 'pecking order', with the largest sharks feeding first. The diet, for large individuals at least, can best be described as anything and everything. Tiger sharks are among the most indiscriminate feeders in the animal kingdom!

The broad, curved, notched, serrated teeth, nearly identical in the upper and lower jaws, give tiger sharks the ability to saw through turtle shell and mammal bone, enabling them to cut live sea turtles in half, or scavenge floating whale carcasses. They will dismember and consume terrestrial mammals that end up in the sea, whether live or dead, including cattle, horses, chickens, rats, pigs, goats, sheep, dogs, monkeys, hyenas, donkeys, and humans. They are important predators on monk seals and dolphins, and also take sea lions, fur seals, and probably porpoises. They swallow venomous sea snakes whole, and iguanas as well. Tiger sharks gather seasonally near sea-bird rookeries, and take fledgling albatrosses and other birds that fall in the water during their first attempts at flight. They also capture wading birds, and land birds that drop to the ocean during migrations. Birds found in the stomachs of tiger sharks include a yellow-billed cuckoo, wood thrushes, cormorants, pelicans and doves. Tiger sharks feed on a variety of fishes, including poisonous varieties such as boxfishes and puffers, but seem to prefer elasmobranchs, although these may be mostly taken when hooked on fishing gear. A wide assortment of sharks and rays, both large and small, have been found in their stomachs, including other tiger sharks. They also consume large numbers of invertebrates, including squid, octopus, crab, lobster, conch, clams, tunicates (sea squirts) and jellyfish.

The reputation of tiger sharks as 'garbage cans with fins', however, stems largely from the reports of inedible garbage found in their stomachs, including almost anything that falls, or is tossed, into the water. Stomach contents reputedly include license plates, chunks of wax, grass, tiles, cardboard, ropes, shoes, raincoats, coal, wood, bottles, barrels, tin cans, a drum, and a birth-control pill container.

There is no question that tiger sharks also partake occasionally of the 'ultimate junk food' – human flesh. In most cases, they merely scavenge bodies of victims of drowning, other accidents, or even foul play. In a celebrated case in 1935 in Australia, a tiger shark captured for an oceanarium regurgitated a tattooed arm, which upon examination turned out to have been severed, not bitten, from the body. The victim was identified from the tattoo, and was found to have been involved in criminal activities with two partners. One of the partners was

Tiger sharks are born with a spotted color pattern, which turns into stripes in older juveniles, and fades to solid gray counter-shading in mature sharks.

found shot to death shortly after the police questioned him. The other partner was charged with the tattooed man's murder. After three trials he was released due to a ruling that murder could not be proven without a body, and an arm did not constitute a body.

In some cases, however, tiger sharks are known to have attacked living swimmers and surfers without provocation. The broad — one might say unlimited — spectrum of their diet makes them a hazard to virtually any living thing in the ocean, and they are deservedly considered among the most dangerous species in tropical and subtropical waters.

Tiger sharks are fished for their meat, which is highly prized, for leather, fins, liver oil, cartilage, sport, revenge, and trophies (the jaws and teeth are valuable as souvenirs and for jewelry). They are also subject to entanglement in shark mesh nets at beaches and are often specifically targeted in 'shark control' campaigns. They often survive when hooked on a set line, and are captured in this way for display in oceanaria, and for use as 'extras' in films. They usually do not survive long in captivity, however. Reportedly, dozens have been sacrificed in the making of a single film of the 'blockbuster' genre. Their conservation status is unknown. They are widespread, but apparently not very common, as evidenced by the lack of success that film-makers and tour operators typically have when trying to attract them for viewing. Tiger sharks are not protected in any country except Israel, which does not allow the killing of any cartilaginous fish.

SPECIES SNAPSHOT: School Shark, Soupfin Shark, or Tope Shark, *Galeorhinus galeus*; Family Triakidae

The soupfin, or tope, shark is a slender, medium-sized hound shark, which is widespread in temperate and subtropical waters, and is found from the shoreline down to depths of 1800 ft (550 m). Also known as the school shark, for its habit of traveling in schools of up to 100 individuals, it is found off both coasts of South America, the west coasts of North America, Africa, and Europe, and around Australia and New Zealand. Topes have a long snout, large eyes, five short gill slits, a second dorsal which is about the same size as the anal fin and much smaller than the first dorsal, and an unusually shaped tail, with a lower lobe that is large for a hound shark and a large 'subterminal lobe' at the tip of the upper lobe. They are brown to gray above, and lighter below.

Topes are active by day and night, and keep swimming most of the time. They feed mostly on bony fishes, but also take squid, octopus, shrimp, crabs, lobsters, snails, worms, and other invertebrates, and occasionally small sharks and rays. They are born at a size of about 1 ft (30 cm) and grow to about 6½ ft (2 m) over a lifespan that can exceed 50 years. They undertake long migrations between summer and winter habitats, and between feeding and breeding areas, traveling as far as 1500 miles (2500 km) at a rate of up to 58 km (35 miles) per day.

Females mature at an age of 8 to 11 years. They seek out shallow bays to give birth to litters of 6 to 52 pups, then rest for 2 to 3 years before breeding again. The bays serve as nursery areas for the pups, which stay there for up to two years before moving off to deeper waters. The reproductive mode is live-bearing with no placenta.

Topes have been heavily exploited throughout their range for meat, fins, leather, oil, and fishmeal, and are also caught for sport. Due to their slow growth, and low rate of reproduction, populations can withstand only very low levels of fishing pressure. The fishery off the west coast of North America collapsed in just over ten years, and has not recovered after nearly half a century. The species is considered highly vulnerable. Juveniles are particularly at risk due to their inshore, shallow-water habitat. Topes have never been implicated in attacks on humans.

Order Hexanchiformes

Contains two families with six species, known as frilled sharks, sixgill sharks, and sevengill sharks. The six- and sevengill sharks are sometimes referred to collectively as cow sharks. There are six or seven gill slits, instead of the usual five, and only one dorsal fin, instead of two. There is an anal fin, which is similar in size to the dorsal fin. The teeth are multicuspid. Reproduction is by live birth without a placenta.

Tope sharks, a type of hound shark also known as school sharks or soupfin sharks, are among the most heavily exploited of all shark species, for food, fins, vitamin oil, and sport. The name derives from the word 'taupe', meaning brownish gray, from the French word for 'mole'.

The bluntnose sixgill shark cannot tolerate bright light, as it is unable to constrict its
pupils. Therefore it usually stays in deep water, like other cow sharks. However, when plankton blooms
darken the waters of British Columbia in late summer, sixgill sharks ascend to shallower depths.

SPECIES SNAPSHOT: Frilled Shark, *Chlamydoselachus anguineus*; Family Chlamydoselachidae

The frilled shark is the only known member of its family. It is known from a number of widely separated locations in the Atlantic, Pacific, and Indian Oceans, mostly from temperate areas, but also from the tropics and subtropics. It may be that the spotty distribution record is due to spotty fishing effort in the deep water where it lives, and from its refusal to take baited hooks. It is normally found on deep shelves and slopes from 400–4200 ft (120–1280 m), but is occasionally caught at the surface. It is also known as the eel shark, both for its dark, eel-like body, and for the eel-like appearance of its head, with the mouth at the end of the short snout (rather than underneath the snout, as in the cow sharks and most others). The six long gill slits have frilled margins. The first pair of gill slits are joined underneath, and nearly encircle the head. The pectoral fins are short and rounded. The single dorsal fin is placed far back, and is the smallest of the fins – even smaller than the anal and pelvic fins. The caudal (tail) fin is long and flexible. Some scientists consider the frilled shark to be the most primitive living shark, because its teeth are very similar to the phoebodont sharks, which lived almost 400 MYA.

Frilled sharks are born at a size of about 16–22 in (40–55 cm) and grow to a length of almost 6½ ft (2 m). Females mature at a size of about 4½ ft (1.4 m), and bear litters of 2 to 12 pups, after a gestation period that may be up to three-and-a-half years. If that estimate is correct, it is the longest gestation of any known vertebrate. Although there is no placenta, it is suspected that the embryos receive nutrients from the mother in some fashion during the latter part of the pregnancy. The diet is mostly squid, and some fish, which are probably impaled on the pitchfork-like teeth, and swallowed whole. The teeth have a broad base, and three long, slender, pointed cusps.

Frilled sharks were once fished for meat and fishmeal in Japan, but are now only taken as bycatch in bottom trawls. Population size and status are unknown. They pose no threat to humans.

SPECIES SNAPSHOT: Bluntnose Sixgill Shark, *Hexanchus griseus*; Family Hexanchidae

The bluntnose sixgill is distinguished from the bigeye sixgill by growing about two-and-a-half times as long, by smaller eyes, and a broader snout. Both are gray to brown, lighter underneath, and have a single dorsal fin, placed well back, which is moderately small, about the same size as the anal fin. The upper lobe of the tail is much longer than the lower. The bluntnose is found around the world in both temperate and tropical seas, from the surface to depths of at least 6150 ft (1875 m). Juveniles are more likely to be found inshore. Adults are usually in depths greater than 300 ft (90 m), but sometimes ascend to shallower depths where surface waters are cold and dark, notably in British Columbia. They are primarily nocturnal, and avoid bright lights.

Sixgills have unusual teeth. The uppers are dagger-like, while the lower teeth are like sawblades. This combination, and their large size, gives bluntnose sixgills the ability to prey upon a wide variety of organisms, both small and large, including crabs, shrimp, squid, marine mammals, and many kinds of fishes, including herring, flounders and swordfish, rays, chimaeras, and other sharks. The diet changes as the shark grows.

Bluntnose sixgills are born at a size of about 24–28 in (60–70 cm), and grow to over 16 ft (4.8 m). Females mature at about 15 ft (4.5 m) and bear litters of 22 to 108 pups.

Sixgill sharks are fished for meat, fishmeal, oil, and sport, and are also taken as bycatch in longline fisheries. Population sizes and status are unknown. They are not known to attack humans without provocation. The shallow population near Vancouver Island is an attraction for scuba divers. The sharks often appear oblivious of the divers unless they are touched, or a strobe light is fired at close range, in which case they may bolt, or snap. Bluntnose sixgill sharks are locally protected in the waters of British Columbia, Canada.

Order Squaliformes

Contains seven families with 113 species, known as dogfish, bramble sharks, gulper sharks, velvet sharks, plunket sharks, kitefin sharks, lantern sharks, tail light sharks, pygmy sharks, cigar sharks, cookie cutter sharks, sleeper sharks, Greenland sharks, spurdogs, and rough sharks. The body is roughly cylindrical, with a conical snout. There are two dorsal fins, with or without spines, and no anal fin. There are five gill slits, a spiral valve in the intestine, and nictitating membranes on the eyes. Members of this order are most numerous in the deep sea, but range all over the globe from the Arctic to Antarctic, and from the surface down to over 20,000 ft (6000 m). They range in size from less than 8 in (20 cm) to over 20 ft (6 m). Reproduction is live-bearing without placenta, in all species for which the reproductive mode is known.

SPECIES PROFILE: Spiny Dogfish or Piked Dogfish, *Squalus acanthias*; Family Squalidae

The spiny dogfish is well known due to extensive fisheries that have supplied it as the main ingredient in 'fish and chips' for many years. It is an abundant small to medium-sized shark with a worldwide distribution in temperate to boreal waters from the surface to a depth of at least 3000 ft (900 m). It occurs both inshore and offshore, but usually in association with the bottom. The upper body is gray, often with sparse white spots, and the underside is pale. There is a large crescent spiracle above and behind the large eye. A sharp, mildly venomous spine precedes both dorsal fins.

Spiny dogfish are born at a size of 8–12 in (20–30 cm) and can grow to 5 ft (1.5 m) over the course of a life that can last 70 years, but most are not more than 39 in (1 m) in length. They form schools of up to thousands of individuals, which are segregated by size and sex. They may be the most numerous sharks in the world. They are highly migratory, and move up and down coasts with the seasons, following food sources both offshore, and into shallow bays and estuaries, even into brackish water. Some individuals are found alone, or in schools of other sharks, such as brown smoothhounds or leopard sharks.

In addition to their coastwise movements, spiny dogfish migrate both vertically in the water column, and inshore and offshore, in order to stay within their preferred temperature range of 45–59°F (7–15°C). In the northwest Atlantic they move offshore in winter, and feed very little until they return to the coast in the spring. Sharks in some populations make only small movements, while others cross oceans. A dogfish tagged in Washington State was recaptured 3900 miles (6500 km) away in Japan, seven years later.

The teeth are 'clipper-like', with cusps that are angled almost parallel to the gum line. They are capable of dealing with a large variety of prey, and can easily chop up animals too large to be swallowed whole. Young dogfish even attack fish larger than themselves. The diet includes many types of bony fishes, and their eggs. Both schooling midwater fishes and bottom fishes are represented, from fast-swimming mackerels to flatfishes and blennies. They also consume an assortment of invertebrates, including shrimp, crabs, krill, squid, octopus, jellyfish, worms, snails, scallops, and sea cucumbers.

Females mature at a size of 39 in (1 m) or less, and an age of 10 to 36 years. They move into shallow bays and estuaries to give birth to litters of 1 to 20 pups. Embryos are nourished from a yolk sac while developing within the mother, and are born live. The gestation period is 18 to 24 months, the longest known for any elasmobranch, with the possible exceptions of basking sharks and frilled sharks.

Spiny dogfish do not attack humans, but fishers can be injured by the spines. The second dorsal spine can be used as a defensive weapon by thrashing the tail around. Some people are allergic to the toxin associated with the spines, and can have a severe reaction.

Spiny dogfish are heavily fished for meat, oil, pet food, fertilizer, leather, and squalamine, an antibiotic steroid. Large numbers are also caught as bycatch in other fisheries. Natural enemies include seals, orcas, and larger sharks and fishes. The slow growth rate, delayed maturity, long gestation period, and small litter size combine to make this species extremely susceptible to over-exploitation. To make things worse, fisheries often target schools of mature females, because these

Smalltooth sawfish (top left); spiny dogfish or piked dogfish (top right); frilled shark (bottom left); and velvet belly shark (bottom right).

This Pacific angel shark is easy to see because it is swimming a short distance
above the seafloor and casting a shadow on the bottom. In their normal 'ambush' mode, lying
still on the bottom, partially covered with sediment, angel sharks are almost invisible as they scan the
water above them for potential prey. When any object of the correct size passes overhead within striking
distance, the angel shark explodes from the bottom, engulfing it in its rapidly expanding jaws.

are the largest sharks. Most stocks are now considered overfished, and the species is ranked as highly vulnerable.

SPECIES SNAPSHOT: Velvet Belly Shark, *Etmopterus spinax*;
Family Etmopteridae

The velvet belly shark is a medium-sized lantern shark which is found in the Mediterranean and eastern Atlantic, from South Africa to Iceland and Norway. It inhabits depths from 230–6600 ft (70–2000 m), but is most common from 650–1600 ft (200–500 m). It occurs both on and near the bottom, and well up into the water column, usually on outer continental shelves and upper slopes. The photograph on page 107 was taken at the bottom of a Norwegian fjord, at night, at a depth of 260 ft (80 m).

Like other lantern sharks, it has large green eyes, five very short gill slits, a big spiracle, no anal fin, an asymmetrical tail, blunt pectoral fins, and two dorsal fins with spines, the second dorsal and spine larger than the first. Lantern sharks get their name from the small light organs on the underside which are believed to emit a glow that matches the faint light downwelling from the surface in deep water, 'erasing' their silhouette and making them effectively invisible to a predator looking up from below.

The velvet belly shark is distinguished by a black underside, with the appearance of black velvet, and black flank markings above and behind the pelvic fins, and on the tail and tail base. The tail has almost no lower lobe. The upper side is brown, contrasting with the black belly.

Velvet bellies are born at a length of about 4½–5½ in (12–14 cm) and grow to a maximum length of about 2 ft (60 cm). Most are under 1½ ft (45 cm). Sexual maturity is attained at 13–14 in (33–36 cm). Pups develop without a placenta, and are born live, in litters of 6 to 20.

The diet consists of small fishes, squid, and crustaceans. Stomach contents suggest that adults hunt mainly in open water, off the bottom, with most feeding occurring during the day, and reduced hunting activity at night. The upper teeth are designed for piercing and holding, with a pointed primary cusp surrounded by one, two, or occasionally three pairs of shorter cusplets. The lower teeth are designed for cutting, with a single cusp inclined at an oblique angle, presenting a nearly flat edge on the upper surface.

Velvet belly sharks are fished for meat and fishmeal. They appear to be common in European waters, but population sizes and the amount of fishing pressure are both unknown.

Order Squatiniformes

Contains a single family with 18 bottom-dwelling species known as angel sharks. The body is flattened and ray-like, but the pectoral fins are distinct, and not joined to the head to form a disc as in the rays. There are two short spineless dorsal fins, and no anal fin. The caudal fin is small, with the lower lobe larger than the upper. The mouth is at the forward end of the body, not underneath as in rays. The five gill slits face downwards, and are covered by the pectoral fins. The angel sharks are most closely related to rays and saw sharks, and may be ancestral to these groups. Most species prefer cool water and are found either in the temperate-boreal zone, or in deep tropical waters. There is no placenta and pups are born live in all species for which the reproductive mode is known.

SPECIES SNAPSHOT: Pacific Angel Shark, *Squatina californica*;
Family Squatinidae

The Pacific angel shark, sometimes called monk shark or monkfish, was once common in temperate waters of the western coasts of North and South America. It prefers mud and sand bottoms in depths of 10–4,300 ft (3–1320 m). It is white underneath, and sandy to brown or gray on top, with brown flecks and speckles which camouflage it perfectly against the bottom, especially when partially buried. The eyes are fairly large, but are patterned like the body, and are so nearly invisible that it is easy to mistake the two large spiracles behind them for the eyes.

Angel sharks are born at a size of 8–12 in (20–30 cm), and grow as long as 5 ft (1.5 m), over a lifespan of about 35 years. They feed primarily on bottom and near-bottom fishes, and on squid. By day, they are ambush feeders, lying quietly on the bottom, covered with sediment, waiting for something to pass overhead. When a fish swims within a critical distance, the angel shark lunges forward and thrusts open its powerful jaws which are covered with sharp, spiky teeth. By night, angel sharks become more active, and swim over the bottom, feeding on sleeping and unwary fish.

Females mature at about 3 ft (90 cm) and bear litters of 1 to 13 pups after a gestation period of 10 to 12 months. Angel sharks are normally inoffensive, but can give a painful bite if molested.

The Pacific angel shark is heavily fished for meat, and is also taken as bycatch in shrimp, halibut, and other fisheries, and processed for fishmeal. Populations have been severely affected by overfishing.

Order Pristiophoriformes

Contains one family with nine species known as saw sharks. These unusual sharks have a body that is slightly flattened, but not nearly so much as in the angel sharks or the rays, and an elongated snout which is lined on both sides with rostral teeth, and has the appearance (and function) of a sword. The body form and rostral armament are so bizarre that one could suppose them to be odd evolutionary experiments, except that a group of rays known as sawfishes have a very similar body design, and almost identical weaponry. The saw sharks are more closely related to the rays than to any other group of sharks, but whether they are most closely related to sawfish is uncertain. Experts have yet to determine whether the similarities they share are due to a direct evolutionary link, or to convergent evolution, i.e. two groups of animals that started out looking different, but evolved similar features in response to similar environmental demands. The most obvious characteristic that distinguishes saw sharks from sawfishes is the set of long barbels, or 'whiskers', which protrude from the rostrum well forward of the nostrils. The body is less flattened than in sawfishes, and the gill slits are on the side, rather than underneath. The rostral teeth of sawfish are all the same length, whereas those of saw sharks are of assorted sizes. Saw sharks are capable of replacing their rostral teeth if lost, but sawfish are not.

Saw sharks have two fairly large dorsal fins, without spines, and no anal fin. The tail has an elongated upper lobe only. There are five or six pairs of gill slits. They occupy mud, sand, and gravel bottoms, usually in deep water, but can be found at shallow depths in some cold water areas (sawfishes are more tropical). The saw is believed to be used both to disable prey by slashing back and forth through schools of fish, and to dig in the bottom for crabs and other buried quarry. There is also a set of sharp teeth in both jaws for holding prey.

SPECIES SNAPSHOT: Longnose Saw Shark, *Pristiophorus cirratus*; Family Pristiophoridae

The longnose saw shark, or common saw shark, is known only from the southern coast of Australia. It is found on sand and gravel bottoms from close inshore to depths of over 1000 ft (300 m). It is white underneath, and tan to brown above with a pattern of darker brown markings. There are five short gill slits. The barbels are midway between the mouth and the tip of the rostrum. Large individuals have denticles covering the dorsal and pectoral fins, whereas these fins are scaleless in other species. The denticles covering the rest of the body are quite small, giving the skin a smooth texture.

Common saw sharks are born at a length of 11–15 in (27–38 cm), and grow to at least 4½ ft (1.4 m). They are known to live at least 15 years. They swim close to the bottom, trailing their barbels along the sand to locate buried fish and crustaceans, then use the 'saw' to dig them out and whack them.

Pups are born live, after a year-long gestation period during which they derive most of their nutrition from an extremely large yolk sac. The litters of 3 to 22 pups are born in shallow coastal areas.

Longnose saw sharks are fished for food. They are harmless to humans unless handled, in which case they may use the snout as a defensive weapon.

The long barbels hanging from the rostrum of this longnose saw shark and the
uneven tooth length on the saw identify it clearly as a saw shark, rather than a sawfish. Also,
the gills are visible on the side of the head, whereas they are underneath in sawfish.

*Cownose rays (Rhinoptera bonasus) are found along the east coasts of North
and South America, and in the Gulf of Mexico. They form schools of up to hundreds of individuals,
which are segregated by size and sex. They feed on lobsters, crabs and mollusks.*

Order Rajiformes (Batoidea)

Contains nine suborders with 20 families, and 627 species, known as skates, rays, sawfish, guitarfish, mantas, mobulas, devilfish, numbfish, wedgefish, violinfish, stingarees, etc. The terms 'batoid elasmobranchs' or just 'rays' apply to the group as a whole. The body is flattened, as an adaptation to a bottom-dwelling existence. The pectoral fins are fused with the head and body. There is no anal fin. The five or six gill slits are located on the underside. Skates reproduce by laying leathery egg cases on the bottom. All other batoids are live-bearing, with nourishment of the developing embryo by uterine fluid, enabling the offspring to be born at a weight sometimes 50 times greater than that of the fertilized egg. The batoids are believed to be closely allied with the angel sharks (Squatiniformes) and saw sharks (Pristiophoriformes).

SPECIES PROFILE: Manta Ray, *Manta birostris*; Family Mobulidae

Manta rays are found worldwide in the tropics and subtropics, from close inshore to the open ocean, occasionally venturing into temperate waters. They are usually seen at or close to the surface, but may also descend to unknown depths. They have, in the past, been classified into a number of different species. These are currently considered invalid, and only one species is recognized. Most experts believe that more than one species does exist, but they have not yet been able to agree on how to differentiate the separate species. Mantas have diamond-shaped bodies, which are black to brown on top, often with paler shoulder patches, and vary from white to patterned to black underneath. Individuals can usually be recognized by the distinctive patterns of dark blotches on the underside. The tail is short and thin, and has no stinging barbs. There is a single small dorsal fin near the base of the tail.

Mantas are the largest of the batoid fishes, yet subsist upon the smallest prey. Mantas and the closely related devil rays in the genus *Mobula* are the only rays which consume plankton by filter feeding. In order to take advantage of this abundant food source, they have secondarily evolved from the bottom-dwelling lifestyle characteristic of most rays back to a pelagic lifestyle more typical of the sharks from which rays evolved.

Since their sedentary ancestors left them with only a thin whip of a tail, mantas cannot use their tails for propulsion, as do most pelagic fishes. Instead, they flap their pectoral fins, which remain fused to the body and head, but have extended out to form broad 'wings', giving the body a delta shape, similar to modern fighter planes, and this is not by coincidence. The hydrodynamic lift provided by a current flowing over a manta's body is sufficient to keep it suspended in the water column with no effort expended. The superb hydrodynamics of the manta's body enable it to avoid sinking without needing the large oily liver which provides buoyancy for many sharks.

The eyes have moved from the top of the head back around to the sides – a more appropriate position for pelagic life, so that the manta can see predators approaching from all directions. The spiracles are small and inconspicuous.

Just forward of the eyes are two 'cephalic lobes' (extensions of the pectoral fins), which are rolled up when the animal is not feeding, and look like horns protruding from the front of the head. During feeding, the 'horns' unroll and act as scoops to funnel plankton into the wide, gaping mouth. The mouth is at the forward end of the body, unlike the mobulas, which have their mouths set back a short distance below the snout. Plankton, mostly small crustaceans, and possibly small fish in some cases, are filtered out with complex filtering plates inside the five large gill slits. There are 130–200 rows of small, pebble-like vestigial teeth in a band on the lower jaw, which may be covered with skin, and no teeth in the upper jaw. Mantas are often solitary, but may also occur in small groups. Where plankton is concentrated, dozens may be seen feeding in close proximity.

Manta rays are born at about 4 ft (1.2 m) disc width, and a weight of about 20 lbs (9 kg) and grow to a width of about 22 ft (6.7 m). Large specimens can weigh over two tons. Usually a single pup is born at a time, at an interval of 2 to 3 years. It is probable that only the left ovary develops, as is the case with mobula rays that have been studied. Reports that mantas supposedly give birth while breaching appear to be based on a single description of a manta that aborted its fetus during a breach while struggling to escape after being harpooned. The gestation period is unknown, as is the lifespan, although mantas are believed to be long-lived. During the mating season, 'trains' of mantas can be seen, consisting of a female followed by several to more than a dozen males. Mating has been filmed, with a pair in a belly-to-belly position and the male holding the pectoral fin of the much larger female in its mouth.

Mantas are frequently accompanied by one to many remoras, which may benefit the manta by eating external parasites, but also produce drag as they 'hitch a ride', and often leave marks where they attach. Mantas also frequent 'cleaning stations' where reef fish swim out to remove parasites. Juvenile mantas sometimes jump clear of the water, but cannot jump as high as their smaller cousins, the mobulas, which are able to clear the water by several body lengths. Adult mantas only drive their bodies part way out of the water before falling back. It is unknown whether this serves to dislodge parasites, or any other purpose.

Mantas have the largest brains of any elasmobranch. A counter-current heat exchange system has been found in the blood vessels surrounding the brain. This is believed to warm the brain, possibly to protect the nervous system against thermal shock when mantas descend suddenly from warm surface waters to cooler waters beneath.

Manta rays are fished for their flesh, and for shark bait, primarily in Mexico, and are also subject to entanglement and capture in nets and other fishing gear set for other species. Very little is known about population sizes and dynamics, making it impossible to assess their current status, but, due to their wide distribution, they are not believed to be at risk, apart from some specific local populations.

Mantas are commonly presumed to be completely nomadic, due to their habit of appearing in certain locations on a sporadic basis. However, the recent advent of long-term observations by scuba divers is beginning to provide strong indications that there are at least some populations which are either locally site-attached or have specific home ranges, or at least a regular migration route. Mantas identified by ventral markings have been repeatedly resighted over periods of years at some locations, and at least one individual was observed on a near-nightly basis at a specific location for several years. This raises the possibility that distinct populations could be easily wiped out by even modest fishing pressure, considering their low reproductive rate.

A marine biologist in a 1969 book laments that mantas which were once common off Florida's Gulf coast, were already rare at that time (just before relating how her team harpooned and 'bang-sticked' a manta that they knew was too large to capture). Another biologist in a 1916 article describes harpooning five mantas and 75 mobulas off the Carolina coast for museum collections. A former president of the National Geographic Society, in a 1965 book describing his successful pleasure hunt for mantas in the Bahamas, makes it clear that they were once sufficiently numerous there to entice sportsmen to journey there specifically to kill them, although they are rarely seen in the Bahamas today. These narratives are illustrated with enough mentions and illustrations of other specimens caught by sports-fishers and sufficient accounts of the ease with which a manta is harpooned, to give plausibility to the assumption that the extreme rarity of manta sightings in U.S. east coast and Gulf waters, and the Bahamas, in the present day, may be at least partially attributed to the abundance of sportsmen, and to a lesser extent, biologists, in those same waters during the first two-thirds of the twentieth century.

Mantas are harmless to humans, unless attacked, when their sheer bulk and power can become a concern. In areas where they are not molested they often exhibit a great deal of curiosity about divers, and may even solicit tactile contact. Gentle scratching (especially on the underside) may mimic the sensations invoked when cleaner-fish remove external parasites.

The offshore variety of manta ray is larger than the inshore one, and has more black pigment. It may one day be recognized as a separate species.

SPECIES SNAPSHOT: Smalltooth Sawfish, *Pristis pectinata*; Family Pristidae
Also known as the broad sawfish, the smalltooth sawfish has a wide, but disjunct, distribution in a broad band on both sides of the equator. Its occurrence in the Pacific Ocean is uncertain, but it is present in the Atlantic and Indian Oceans, the Caribbean, Mediterranean and Red Seas, the Gulf of Mexico, and the Gulf of Carpentaria in Australia. It is

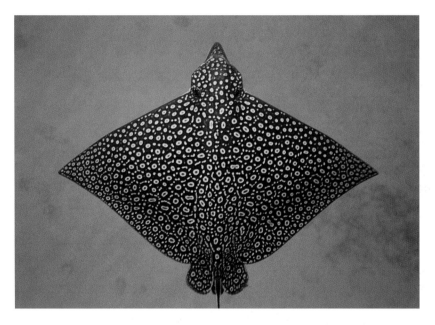

*Spotted eagle ray (*Aetobatus narinari*), a typical batoid elasmobranch.*

primarily marine, but enters lagoons and estuaries to give birth and may even enter lakes and rivers.

The body is intermediate in appearance between a shark and a ray, with two large erect dorsal fins, distinct pectoral fins, and a powerful tail which propels the fish by lateral undulations of the rear half of the body. The lower lobe of the caudal fin is less than half the length of the upper. There is no anal fin. The five gill slits are on the underside, just where the pectoral fins join the head and body. The color is white underneath and gray (sometimes with a shade of blue or green) above. For differences between sawfishes and saw sharks, see the section on Pristiophoriformes on page 110.

The smalltooth sawfish is the largest of the sawfishes, growing from a birth size of about 2 ft (60 cm) to a maximum of about 24 ft (7.6 m). Its 24 to 34 pairs of evenly spaced rostral teeth are smaller and more numerous than those of the largetooth sawfish. Pups are born live, in litters of 15 to 20. At birth the snout is flexible, and the rostral teeth are sheathed in skin to prevent injury to the mother.

It feeds mostly on small fishes, but also on crustaceans and other invertebrates, which it digs from the bottom with its saw. It swings the saw from side to side to impale fish, then scrapes them off against the bottom before eating them.

Sawfish were once common, but have been heavily overfished for meat, liver oil, fins, curios (the saw), and aquarium display specimens. Because of the shape of the rostrum, and their preference for near-shore areas which are subject to high levels of human activity, they are extremely susceptible both to incidental catch in nets set for other species, and to habitat destruction. The smalltooth sawfish is classified by the IUCN as endangered on a worldwide basis, and critically endangered in the NE and SW Atlantic. Once common in U.S. waters, it is now extremely rare. It poses no threat to humans, except when being handled. Sawfishes are legally protected in U.S. Atlantic and Gulf coast waters, and in Indonesia.

SPECIES SNAPSHOT: Cortez Electric Ray; *Narcine entemedor*;
Family Narcinidae
The Cortez electric ray, also known as the lesser electric ray, is found on sandy bottoms in the eastern Pacific from the Sea of Cortez to Panama. It is tan to brown on top and white underneath. The skin is smooth and free of denticles. There are two equal-sized dorsal fins, only slightly smaller than the caudal fin, and no anal fin. The large spiracles are just behind the eyes.

Two primary electric organs on either side of the head are used for defensive purposes. This family of rays can emit discharges of up to only about 37 volts, whereas the torpedo rays (Torpedinidae) can give off discharges of over 100, and possibly 200, volts. A set of

Cortez electric ray with red-tailed triggerfish (top left);
thornback ray feeding on squid egg cases (bottom left); and bat ray in kelp forest (right).

secondary electric organs, behind the primaries, emit much lower voltages, which are believed to be used for communication within the species.

Cortez electric rays rest on the bottom, often covered with sediment, by day, and move into shallow water to feed at night. The prey is mostly small invertebrates, including worms and sea squirts. They are born at a length of 4–5 in (11–12 cm) and grow to a maximum size of about 30 in (76 cm). They are live-bearing, with litters of 4 to 15.

Bottom-dwelling rays are subject to incidental capture in shrimp trawls. Population size and status are unknown. They are not capable of inflicting injury on humans, but can deliver a mild electric shock if molested.

SPECIES SNAPSHOT: White-spotted Shovelnose Ray, *Rhynchobatus djiddensis*; Family Rhynchobatidae

The white-spotted shovelnose ray, or white-spotted guitarfish, is usually found on sandy bottoms, from the shoreline to at least 165 ft (50 m). It inhabits tropical and warm temperate waters of the Indo-Pacific from the Red Sea to New Caledonia, north to Japan, and south to New South Wales and South Africa. It is primarily a marine species, but enters lagoons and estuaries and has been recorded from fresh water in south-east Asia.

The white-spotted guitarfish is the largest member of the family known as 'sharkfin guitarfishes' for the two large shark-like dorsal fins (without spines). The pectoral fins are semi-distinct from the body disc. There is no anal fin, and the upper and lower lobes of the caudal fin are almost equal. The tail is thick and muscular and propels the ray with shark-like side-to-side undulations. The swimming style and somewhat shark-like body have earned these fishes the other common name of 'shark rays'.

The white-spotted shovelnose ray is white underneath and tan to brown above, with small spines on the back, and white spots, which may be absent in larger individuals. It has a triangular snout and two prominent skin folds on the rear margin of the large spiracles, which are just behind the eyes.

The white-spotted shovelnose ray is born at a length of 17–24 in (43–60 cm) and can grow to at least 10 ft (3 m). It feeds on crabs, lobsters, clams, and small fishes. The many small blunt teeth are useful for crushing the shells of small invertebrates. Litters of up to ten pups are delivered live in shallow inshore areas.

It is fished for human consumption, for sport, for use in animal feeds, and in industrial and pharmaceutical products. It is commonly taken as bycatch in trawl nets and drift nets. Size and status of populations are unknown. It is harmless to humans, and usually shy of divers.

SPECIES PROFILE: Blue-spotted Fantail Ray, *Taeniura lymma*; Family Dasyatidae

Also known as the blue-spotted ribbontail ray, this species is common in shallow waters of the tropical Indo-West Pacific from South Africa to the Solomon Islands, including the Red Sea. It can be found from the intertidal zone to a depth of at least 65 ft (20 m). It is common around coral reefs, where it shelters under ledges and in caves at low tide, moving inshore to feed in shallow sandy areas on rising tides. It belongs to the family of whiptail stingrays, which have long thin tails, with venomous barbs, and flattened heads completely fused with the pectoral fins and body to form a disc that is round to rhomboidal in shape. Swimming is accomplished by undulations of the disc margin. There are five gill slits on the underside, and a large spiracle just behind and beneath each eye. The mouth has many small teeth.

The blue-spotted ribbontail ray has a smooth oval disc, which can be tan to yellow-green, decorated with bright blue polka dots. A bright blue stripe runs along each side of the tail, from the base to the tip. There are usually two barbs, also blue. A blue skin fold running down the underside of the tail, from just forward of the barbs to the

The white-spotted shovelnose ray (top) and blue-spotted ribbontail stingray (bottom) illustrate the tremendous diversity of form and color among rays.

tip of the tail, is responsible for the names 'ribbontail' or 'fantail' ray.

This species should not be confused with the blue-spotted stingray, or blue-spotted maskray, *Dasyatis kuhlii*, which belongs to the same family, and has a similar distribution. The maskray has a rhomboidal disc, which is brown to tan with fewer and paler blue spots, and does not have blue tail stripes. The skin fold under the tail is more narrow than that of the fantail ray, and does not reach the tip of the tail. There is also a short fin fold on the top of the tail (absent in the fantail ray). Neither the skin folds nor the barbs are blue. There are dark bands around the tail, and a dark bar is sometimes visible across the eyes.

Blue-spotted fantail rays feed on small mollusks, shrimps, crabs, worms, and fishes, which they find buried in the sand. They are known to be active by day, but may also feed at night. When not feeding, they frequently visit cleaning stations to have parasites removed by cleaner wrasses. Reproduction is live-bearing, with about seven young per litter.

This species is of little interest to fisheries, but is frequently encountered by divers. It is shy and unaggressive, but well-armed with two spines sheathed in tissue served by venom glands. Reports of serious injuries to humans are, however, extremely rare. Since these rays hide under coral and in caves, and rarely bury themselves under sand, the chance of a person stepping on one accidentally is much less than for other members of the family. The vibrant coloration is in stark contrast to the cryptic colors of most other stingrays. Many animals that sport flashy colors are extremely poisonous or venomous and use the colors to advertise that fact, but this species seems much less of a hazard than many other stingrays, and usually flees rather than attacking. It may be that the bright color pattern is primarily for species recognition, and was able to develop because the coral reef habitat allows the fantail rays to hide themselves in a safe hole, rather than depending upon camouflaging themselves against a sand background, like most stingrays.

SPECIES SNAPSHOT: Bat Ray, *Myliobatis californica*; Family Myliobatidae

The bat ray is found along the west coast of North America, from Oregon to the Sea of Cortez, from the surface to depths of 165 ft (50 m). It belongs to the family of eagle rays, or duck-bill rays, which have a diamond-shaped body disc, wider than it is long, and a head that is partially distinct from the disc. Propulsion is by flapping of the pectoral 'wings'. The snout has a projecting lobe which looks like, and is used as, a plow. The teeth are broad and flat, and fused into plates. The long, filamentous tail has a small dorsal fin near its base.

Bat rays are brown to olive to almost black on top and white underneath. The 'bill' is broad and rounded, like a shovel. There are five short venomous spines just behind the base of the tail. They are born at a width of about 1 ft (30 cm) and grow to about 6 ft (1.8m) over a lifespan of at least 23 years. They spend much of their time on the bottom, either resting in depressions, or grubbing for buried prey. The diet, which changes with age, includes clams, oysters, abalone, worms, crabs, shrimp, snails, and small bony fishes. In addition to plowing food out of the bottom with the rostrum, they sometimes expose it by balancing on the tips of the pectoral fins and pumping the body up and down to create a depression in the sand. Hard mollusks are crushed and spit out. Then the soft parts are selectively reingested.

Bat rays can be solitary or schooling. Seasonal mating aggregations can number in the hundreds. In the late afternoon, courting rays flock near the surface. Males slip underneath females and swim with synchronized movements, using spines above the eyes to grasp the female's underside while swimming in a back to belly position. One clasper is then rotated upwards to mate. Two to five pups are born live after a gestation period of 9 to 12 months. Females reach maturity at an age of about five years, and a width of about 3 ft (90 cm).

Bat rays are fished commercially in Mexico. Natural enemies include sevengill sharks, other large sharks and orcas and sea lions. Bat rays are shy and harmless to humans, except when handled.

*The Pacific torpedo ray (*Torpedo californica*) uses a high-voltage electric discharge for both feeding and defense.*

Swimming with Sharks

As old phobias about sharks and rays have been replaced by an appreciation of these creatures as fascinating and attractive wildlife, more and more people have developed an interest in viewing these impressive animals in their natural habitat. Generally this requires certification and experience with the use of scuba gear, although in some cases a mask and snorkel are adequate. A number of species are now maintained in captivity at various aquariums around the world, where they can be observed by non-swimmers. To see elasmobranchs in the wild, it is not necessary to sign up for any special tour. They can be seen in almost any salt water environment, and some fresh water habitats as well. Especially in the Indo-Pacific, a variety of small to medium-sized species may be encountered on and around coral reefs where most dives are conducted. However, the probability of seeing a particular species is much higher on a special excursion. Shark- and ray-viewing tours have become an important factor in conservation, by providing an economic incentive which may be the only force strong enough to prevent the extermination of these interesting animals from some areas. In one location it was estimated that each shark at a certain reef attracted an average of U.S. $100,000 annually in revenues to local businesses.

In general, elasmobranchs, like most wild animals, are timid creatures which tend to avoid humans whenever possible. There are exceptions – a few special places where elasmobranchs can be reliably encountered under natural circumstances. But in most cases, to get more than a fleeting glance, it is necessary to attract the animals into the vicinity of the viewer. This is usually done by placing food in the water. This is a controversial practice, which has been criticized on grounds of both safety and alteration of the animals' natural behavior. Nonetheless many thousands of people have enjoyed baited shark and ray dives, and they continue to be offered at an increasing number of locations. This book will not enter the debate about whether such activities are safe or proper, but will include, in this chapter, information about how and where various shark and ray viewing activities are conducted, and how to participate without unnecessary risk. The listing of locations and species for which tours are available will be, by necessity, incomplete, as new encounters are being developed all the time.

All Encounters

Every situation is different. Therefore the one rule that is always important to follow before going into the ocean to look for sharks or rays is to pay careful attention to the instructions given by the guide. Every excursion into the water carries with it a certain amount of risk due to currents, motor vehicles, and other hazards which can be quite different in one location from another. The behavior of sharks also varies from place to place, even for the same species, and different protocols are followed for the encounters offered by different operators. To avoid getting into trouble, it is always necessary to follow the instructions given for any particular tour. Ask questions if the instructions are not clear.

A few general suggestions apply to most situations: dress appropriately. Wear a full wet suit or at least a dive-skin, and gloves. Bare skin is subject to abrasion injuries from dermal denticles. Dark colors are almost always best. Most sharks are fish-eaters, and are attracted to light colors, such as white and yellow, which are similar in tone to the belly of a fish. (Exceptions are species which hunt by looking for dark silhouettes, such as great whites.) Do not swim at sharks. Regardless of whether it is a baited or non-baited situation, it is better to let the animal come to you. A timid animal can be easily frightened away by a direct approach. A bold animal may respond aggressively to the provocation. Keep hands down, and still. And, of course, it is never a good idea to touch a wild animal.

If a shark begins to display an excessive degree of interest, the best response is usually to move slowly away from it. Dr Erich Ritter, who studies shark–human interactions, suggests moving in a direction about 90° away from the direction the shark is traveling in. Turning sideways to a shark shows it the full size of your body, which is more intimidating than moving directly away from it. He also recommends against ascending immediately, unless the boat is close and directly above. If the shark continues to pursue too closely, he suggests holding out a stick or other object to keep it from coming closer. If necessary, it can be pushed gently away with a gloved hand, stick, camera, etc. The gills are the most sensitive area. It may not even be necessary to touch the shark. Just the sensation of water pressure on the gills will often be sufficient to make it turn away. Hitting a shark aggressively is likely to produce an aggressive response. Dr Ritter points out that when confronted with a large unfamiliar object in their environment, sharks are more likely to evaluate it as a potential threat than to consider it as a food source. Aggressive actions may provoke a shark to defend itself or its 'space'. (Sharks have not been shown to have fixed territories, but members of some species will defend an area around themselves which may vary in size according to circumstances.) Photographers should be aware that strobe units create an electric field that may attract a shark's interest. If it comes too close for comfort, it might be a good idea to switch the strobe off.

A shark should never be surrounded, or have its escape route cut off, for example by blocking the exit from a cave. Sharks and rays, like many wild animals, use 'body language' to communicate with each other, and may use species-specific threat displays to warn other animals to back off. In southern stingrays, this threat is unmistakable: the rear part of the body is raised, with the stinger curved forward, ready to strike. In sharks, the signals may be less obvious to our eyes, but are equally important to heed. Biologist Richard Martin has observed threat displays in 22 different species of sharks. According to his and Dr Ritter's observations, a typical display involves a lowering of the pectoral fins, a stiffening of the muscles, which is very noticeable in the tail, and a change in swimming style, often with a shortening of the side-to-side tail sweeps. The swimming may begin to appear jerky, and less efficient. The pectoral fins are also lowered in normal swimming course adjustments, but in such adjustments, they are only depressed briefly, and often held at different angles on the two sides of the body. When used as a threat display, they are held stiffly down for an extended period, at about the same angle on both sides.

One of the most dramatic threat displays is performed by the gray reef shark. In its most intense form, the entire body is bent into an S-curve with the back arched, the snout up, and the pectoral fins down. The shark then swims slowly while 'waggling' from side to side. If the threat to which the shark is responding is not removed, it will charge and bite. Attacks have been elicited deliberately, by pursuing reef sharks with a small submarine until they reacted defensively, and accidentally, by discharging a flash unit while photographing a displaying shark.

In most situations divers have very little to fear from sharks or rays, but should afford them the same respect accorded to any wild animal. A number of divers have received painful injuries by such actions as pulling on the tail of a resting nurse shark, angel shark, or wobbegong, grabbing at stingrays, etc. 'I would never say that sharks are harmless', says Ritter, 'but they are pussycats compared to tigers, lions, and crocodiles. The aggressiveness is mainly played in our heads'.

Baited Encounters

In baited encounters, it is particularly important to pay careful attention to the briefing, and follow instructions from the dive leader. The sharks in these situations are conditioned to follow a certain routine in order to obtain food. If the pattern is disrupted, they may become confused. In all circumstances, it is critical to be aware of where the bait is and avoid getting between a shark and its food. It is especially important not to get down-current of the bait, in the scent trail or 'chum line'. Sharks are likely to sample anything encountered inside the scent trail, and being sampled is not part of the fun. In baited dives, divers can often choose their own danger or excitement

*If approached gently, manta rays allow close contact, and even seem to enjoy getting
their bellies tickled lightly, which may mimic the sensation of cleaner-fish at work. They usually flee
when chased or grabbed and may suffer skin infections from rough or frequent contact.*

level by positioning themselves at a distance from the bait which corresponds to their own comfort zone. Sport divers should never attempt to conduct these dives on their own. Providing food to wild animals is an art which requires a learning phase on the part of both the animals and the humans. There is no place for amateurs in shark feeding.

There are many variations on baited encounters. Cage dives are perhaps the safest, although not entirely without hazard. Most cages are not shark-proof, but merely provide a tactile and visual barrier between the sharks and the divers. The cage also serves as a reference point which keeps the divers in one place relative to boat and bait, and prevents sharks from approaching undetected from behind. There are often openings for viewing and photography that are large enough to permit a small shark to enter. Divers must often swim unprotected through open water to get into and out of the cage.

In other dives, the bait is presented to the sharks by a feeder, who may use a spear or similar tool to distribute the food, or present it by hand or even by holding it in the mouth. The latter two methods have resulted in some serious injuries to the feeders, and are much less popular nowadays. In most cases, steel-mesh gloves or suits are now used for hand-feeding. Only in the case of relatively docile species such as stingrays and nurse sharks are guests permitted to handle the bait. And even in these cases it can lead to trouble. Visitors who take bait to 'Stingray City' in the Cayman Islands sometimes end up with bruises from stingrays sucking on their skin in an attempt to find bait which they can smell, but not see.

There are a number of methods by which bait is offered remotely. Such methods avoid having the sharks associate the food with the divers. The bait may be hidden under a coral head, placed in a sealed container which is opened by a pull cord, lowered from a boat in an open container, etc. Perhaps the most innovative variation is the 'chumsicle' method employed at Walker's Cay in the Bahamas. In this technique the bait is mixed with water and frozen around a metal bar which is both anchored to the bottom and suspended from a float, so that the bait is positioned in mid water. If all goes to plan, the bait thaws slowly, and the sharks are able to remove a bit at a time, keeping their interest for an extended period without provoking a frenzy. An air pocket in the chumsicle, however, can cause it to disintegrate prematurely, producing a spectacular and chaotic scene as dozens of sharks rush in at once to compete for the food. At such moments, divers who have positioned themselves too close to the bait source may regret their brashness.

The sharks at all such feeds, however, seem to learn quickly that divers are neither a threat nor a food source. Injuries to divers have been relatively few, mostly minor, and accidental. In stark contrast, injuries to spear-fishers seem to be more common, more serious, and often intentional. The contrast is particularly dramatic in the Bahamas, where a large number of dive operations that offer shark feeding have an excellent safety record, but there are regular reports of serious injuries and even fatalities caused to spear-fishers by the same species of shark (Caribbean reef shark). The difference is likely due to the fact that spear-fishers are dealing with sharks that have not been habituated to divers, and that the fishers are competing directly with the sharks for the food. Additionally, live injured fish are a stronger stimulus to sharks than dead bait.

Whereas only a decade or two ago, very few people had ever seen a shark or ray in its natural habitat, now thousands have experienced this thrill at the locations listed on pages 128–130, or elsewhere. Only locations where the target species are seen on a regular basis are included. Overall, there have been few problems, but there is always risk involved in positioning oneself in close proximity to a large wild animal. Nothing in this book should be taken as a substitute for common sense or for thoroughly investigating any such opportunity before participating.

Divers' bubbles rise around Caribbean reef sharks and blacktip sharks circling the 'chumsicle'. Divers can share the water with up to 200 sharks.

Species	Location	Type of Dive	Comments
Southern Stingray, *Dasyatis americana*	Grand Cayman Island (Caribbean)	baited / snorkel or scuba	
Southern Stingray, *Dasyatis americana*	Ambergris Caye, Belize (Caribbean)	baited / snorkel or scuba	also nurse sharks
Tahitian Stingray, *Himantura fai*	Moorea / French Polynesia (Pacific)	baited / snorkel or scuba	
Manta Ray, *Manta birostris*	San Benedicto Island, Mexico (Pacific)	non-baited / snorkel or scuba	live-aboard boat only; huge mantas
Manta Ray, *Manta birostris*	Yap, Micronesia (Pacific)	non-baited / scuba	divers stay motionless while mantas are cleaned
Manta Ray, *Manta birostris*	Narcondam Island Andaman Islands, India (Andaman Sea)	non-baited / snorkel or scuba	live-aboard boat only; difficult access
Manta Ray, *Manta birostris*	Kona, Hawaii (Pacific)	non-baited / snorkel or scuba	night only; mantas feed on plankton, attracted by lights
Eagle Ray, *Aetobatus narinari*	Caye Caulker, Belize (Caribbean)	baited / snorkel or scuba	one or two rays only
Scalloped Hammerhead, *Sphyrna lewini*	northern Galapagos (E. Pacific)	non-baited / scuba	live-aboard boat only; difficult diving conditions
Scalloped Hammerhead, *Sphyrna lewini*	Cocos Is., Costa Rica (E. Pacific)	non-baited / scuba	live-aboard boat only; difficult diving conditions; also whitetip reef sharks
Scalloped Hammerhead, *Sphyrna lewini*	Malpelo Is., Columbia (E. Pacific)	non-baited / scuba	live-aboard boat only; difficult diving conditions
Scalloped Hammerhead, *Sphyrna lewini*	Layang Layang Atoll, Malaysia (S. China Sea)	non-baited / scuba	somewhat difficult diving conditions also zebra sharks
Scalloped Hammerhead, *Sphyrna lewini*	Sudan (Red Sea)	non-baited / scuba	deep
Scalloped Hammerhead, *Sphyrna lewini*	Sea of Cortez	non-baited / scuba	on sea mounts; deep; not as common as before, due to heavy fishing
Nurse Shark, *Ginglymostoma cirratum*	Marathon, Florida Keys (W. Atlantic)	baited / scuba	
Nurse Shark, *Ginglymostoma cirratum*	Ambergris Caye, Belize (Caribbean)	baited / snorkel or scuba	also stingrays
Tawny Nurse Shark, *Nebrius ferrugineum*	Burma Banks, Thailand (Andaman Sea)	baited / scuba	live-aboard boat only; also silvertips
Silvertip Shark, *Carcharhinus albimarginatus*	Burma Banks, Thailand (Andaman Sea)	baited / scuba	live-aboard boat only; also tawny nurse sharks
Silvertip Shark, *Carcharhinus albimarginatus*	Papua New Guinea (W. Pacific) multiple locations	baited/ scuba	
Silvertip Shark, *Carcharhinus albimarginatus*	Rangiroa, French Polynesia (Pacific)	baited / scuba or snorkel	in open water (off the reef)
Gray Reef Shark, *Carcharhinus amblyrhynchos*	Fiji (Pacific)	baited	
Gray Reef Shark, *Carcharhinus amblyrhynchos*	Santo Espiritu, Vanuatu (Pacific)	baited / scuba	
Gray Reef Shark, *Carcharhinus amblyrhynchos*	Australia (Coral Sea)	baited / scuba	live-aboard boat only; also whitetip reef sharks, blackfin reef sharks
Gray Reef Shark, *Carcharhinus amblyrhynchos*	Palau, Micronesia (Pacific)	non-baited / scuba	active when current is strong

Species	Location	Type of Dive	Comments
Gray Reef Shark, *Carcharhinus amblyrhynchos*	Bikini Atoll, Marshall Islands, Micronesia (Pacific)	baited	observe from boat only; feeding frenzy; unsafe to enter water
Gray Reef Shark, *Carcharhinus amblyrhynchos*	Rangiroa, French Polynesia (Pacific)	baited / scuba	difficult diving conditions
Gray Reef Shark, *Carcharhinus amblyrhynchos*	Moorea, French Polynesia (Pacific)	baited / scuba	also blackfin reef sharks, lemon sharks
Gray Reef Shark, *Carcharhinus amblyrhynchos*	Ras Muhammed, Egypt (Red Sea)	non-baited / scuba	
Gray Reef Shark, *Carcharhinus amblyrhynchos*	Maldives (Indian Ocean)	baited/ non-baited / scuba	shark feeds mostly discontinued but some sharks still hang around
Zebra Shark, *Stegostoma fasciatum* (a.k.a. Leopard Shark)	Layang Layang Atoll, Malaysia (S. China Sea)	non-baited / scuba	somewhat difficult diving conditions; also hammerheads
Zebra Shark, *Stegostoma fasciatum* (a.k.a. Leopard Shark)	Phuket, Thailand (Andaman Sea)	non-baited / scuba	
Caribbean Reef Shark, *Carcharhinus perezi*	Bahamas (W. Atlantic) multiple locations	baited / scuba	
Blacktip Shark, *Carcharhinus limbatus*	Walker's Cay, Bahamas (W. Atlantic)	baited / scuba	dozens; also Caribbean reef sharks; often nurse sharks; sometimes bull sharks and great hammerheads
Blackfin Reef Shark, *Carcharhinus melanopterus*	Moorea, French Polynesia (Pacific)	baited / scuba	also gray reef sharks, lemon sharks
Blackfin Reef Shark, *Carcharhinus melanopterus*	Bora Bora, French Polynesia (Pacific)	baited / scuba or snorkel	also gray reef sharks, lemon sharks
Pacific Lemon Shark, *Negaprion acutidens*	Moorea, French Polynesia (Pacific)	baited / scuba	also gray reef sharks, blackfin reef sharks
Sixgill Shark, *Hexanchus griseus*	Vancouver Island, British Columbia, Canada (N.E. Pacific)	non-baited / scuba	seasonal
Sand Tiger Shark, *Carcharias taurus*	Morehead City, North Carolina (W. Atlantic)	non-baited / scuba	on deep wrecks; somewhat seasonal
Sand Tiger Shark, *Carcharias taurus*	NSW and Queensland, Australia multiple locations	non-baited / scuba	seasonal; also Port Jackson sharks and wobbegongs in NSW
Sand Tiger Shark, *Carcharias taurus*	Ogasawara Islands, Japan (W. Pacific)	non-baited / scuba	seasonal
Sand Tiger Shark, *Carcharias taurus*	South Africa	non-baited / scuba	seasonal
Whitetip Reef Shark, *Triaenodon obesus*	Cocos Is., Costa Rica (E. Pacific)	non-baited / scuba	live-aboard boat only; also hammerheads
Whitetip Reef Shark, *Triaenodon obesus*	Australia (Coral Sea)	non-baited / scuba	live-aboard boat only; divers can participate in research
Horn Shark, *Heterodontus francisci*	California Channel Islands (E. Pacific)	non-baited / scuba	also possibility of angel sharks, leopard sharks, bat rays
Port Jackson Shark, *Heterodontus portusjacksoni*	NSW, Australia, multiple locations	non-baited / scuba	also wobbegongs
Spotted Wobbegong, *Orectilobus maculatus*	NSW, Australia, multiple locations	non-baited / scuba	also Port Jackson sharks

Species	Location	Type of Dive	Comments
Bull (Zambezi) Shark, *Carcharhinus leucas*	Protea Banks, South Africa (Indian Ocean)	baited / scuba	less than 100% certainty
Bull (Zambezi) Shark, *Carcharhinus leucas*	Mozambique, Africa (Indian Ocean)	baited	less than 100% certainty;
Great White Shark	South Africa	baited / scuba	seasonal; cage
Great White Shark	South Australia	baited / scuba	seasonal; cage; also sometimes bronze whalers
Blue Shark, *Prionace glauca*	Southern California, U.S.A. (E. Pacific)	baited / scuba	cage; also sometimes makos
Blue Shark, *Prionace glauca*	Massachusetts, U.S.A. (W. Atlantic)	baited / scuba	cage; seasonal
Blue Shark, *Prionace glauca*	Rhode Island, U.S.A. (W. Atlantic)	baited / scuba	cage; seasonal
Basking Shark, *Cetorhinus maximus*	Isle of Man (Irish Sea)	non-baited / snorkel	seasonal
Oceanic Whitetip, *Carcharhinus longimanus*	Southern Red Sea	non-baited / snorkel or scuba	live-aboard boat only; less than 100% certainty
Oceanic Whitetip, *Carcharhinus longimanus*	Hawaii (Pacific)	non-baited / snorkel or scuba	sometimes follows pilot whales; much less than 100% certainty
Whale Shark, *Rhincodon typus*	Ningaloo Reef W. Australia (Indian Ocean)	snorkel	seasonal
Whale Shark, *Rhincodon typus*	Seychelles (Indian Ocean)	snorkel or scuba	live-aboard boat only; seasonal
Whale Shark, *Rhincodon typus*	South Africa and Mozambique (Indian Ocean)	snorkel or scuba	seasonal
Whale Shark, *Rhincodon typus*	Baja California, Mexico (Sea of Cortez)	snorkel or scuba	seasonal
Whale Shark, *Rhincodon typus*	Donsol, Luzon, Philippines (W. Pacific)	snorkel or scuba	seasonal
Whale Shark, *Rhincodon typus*	Utila, Bay Islands, Honduras (Caribbean)	snorkel or scuba	seasonal
Galapagos Shark, *Carcharhinus galapagensis*	Roca Redonda, Galapagos Islands (E. Pacific)	non-baited / scuba	live-aboard boat only; difficult diving conditions
Sharpnose Shark, *Rhizoprionodon sp.*	Cay Sal Bank, Bahamas (W. Atlantic)	non-baited / scuba	live-aboard boat only; sharks aggregate in 'blue hole'
Silky Shark, *Carcharhinus falciformis*	Nassau, Bahamas (W. Atlantic)	baited / non-baited scuba or snorkel	sharks aggregate around buoy; bait not necessary, but often used
Silky Shark, *Carcharhinus falciformis*	Cocos Is., Costa Rica (E. Pacific)	baited/non-baited scuba or snorkel	live-aboard boat only; sometimes seen by day, feeding on schools of small fish in open water; sometimes attracted with bait by night; also hammerheads, whitetips, sometimes whale sharks, marble rays
Bronze Whaler, *Carcharhinus brachyurus*	Kalbarri, W. Australia (Indian Ocean)	baited	seasonal viewing from boat only at press time (no cage yet)

Recommended Reading

The number of books on sharks must tally in the hundreds. Many are sensationalistic and full of misinformation, or just lacking in much useful information, but a few are excellent. Books on rays are almost non-existent, but they are included with sharks in some of the more recent works. Among the best are the following titles:

Sharks & Rays, The Nature Company Guides, Leighton Taylor, Consultant Editor, Time-Life Books / Weldon Owen, 1997.

Reef Sharks & Rays of the World, by Scott Michael, Sea Challengers, 1993.

Sharks by Doug Perrine, Colin Baxter / Voyageur Press, 1995.

Sharks, Reader's Digest Explorers, Reader's Digest / Weldon Owen, 1998.

Discovering Sharks, Samuel H. Gruber, Editor, American Littoral Society, 1990.

Sharks in Question, by Victor Springer and Joy Gold, Smithsonian Institution Press, 1989.

Sharks and Rays of Australia, by P.R. Last and J.D. Stevens, CSIRO, 1994.

Sharks, John D. Stevens, Consulting Editor, Facts on File / Intercontinental / Weldon Owen, 1987

FAO Species Catalogues – Sharks of the World, by Leonard J.V. Compagno, United Nations Food & Agriculture Organization (new edition expected 1999 or 2000).

Biographical Note

Doug Perrine participated in several shark research cruises while earning his master's degree in marine biology from the University of Miami. He currently resides in Kona, Hawaii, where he manages Innerspace Visions Photography, a stock photo agency specializing in sharks and other marine life.

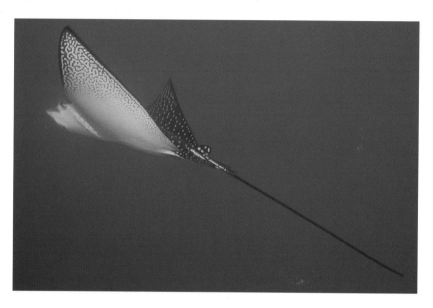

Spotted eagle ray (Aetobatus narinari).

FOR FURTHER INFORMATION CONTACT:

Shark Trust: http://ds.dial.pipex.com/sharktrust/
36 Kingfisher Court, Hambridge Road,
Newbury, Berkshire, RG14 5SJ, UK
Tel: (+44) 01635 551150 / Fax: (+44) 01635 550230
e-mail: sharktrust@naturebureau.co.uk

Shark Foundation: http://www.shark.ch/
Hai-Stiftung
Blütenstrasse 4
CH-8057 Zürich, Switzerland
Tel.: (+41) 1 311 6710 / Fax.: (+41) 1 311 6722
e-mail: shark@shark.ch

Center for Marine Conservation:
http://www.cmc-ocean.org/2_bp/sharkfact.html
1725 DeSales Street, NW
Washington, DC 20036, U.S.A.
Tel: (+1) 202 429 5609 / Fax: (+1) 202 872 0619
email: sonja@dccmc.org

National Coalition for Marine Conservation:
http://www.savethefish.org
3 West Market St.
Leesburg VA 20176, U.S.A.
Tel: (+1) 703 777 0037 / Fax: (+1) 703 777 1107
email: cwilkins22@aol.com

Audubon Society Living Oceans Campaign:
http://www.audubon.org/campaign/lo/
National Audubon Society
Living Oceans Program
550 South Bay Ave.
Islip, NY 11751, U.S.A.
Tel: (+1) 516 224 3369 / Fax: (+1) 516 581 5268
e-mail: mcamhi@audubon.org

Links to a great number of other informational sites about sharks can be found on the Internet at:
http://www.oceanstar.com/shark/links.htm

INDEX

*Entries in **bold** indicate pictures*

Acknowledgments

The author would like to thank the many people who gave of their time and expertise to help in the preparation of this book, including (in no particular order): Marcelo de Carvalho, John Morrissey, Samuel H. Gruber, Giuseppe Notarbartolo-di-Sciara, Rachel Alexander, Ray Troll, Rainer Zangerl, Jose Castro, Reinaldo Caballero, John G. Maisey, Brad Wetherbee, Richard Lund, Eileen Grogan, Gordon Yearsley, Kay Hale, A.J. Kalmijn, Peter Klimley, Enric Cortes, Leonard J.V. Compagno, Scott Eckert, Mike Williams, Mike Coates, Frank Murru, Laurel Gregory, Lisa Diaz, Erich Ritter, Richard Martin, Sarah Fowler, Sonja Fordham, Ivy Rutzky, Dick and Phyllis Dresie, Robert Hueter, Sean Van Sommeran, Marty Snyderman.

Additionally, a note of gratitude is due to the many scientists whose years of research and results published in academic journals form the basis for most of the information presented here, and to the artists and photographers (listed opposite the title page) whose illustrations bring the subject matter to life.